IPM HANDBOOK FOR GOLF COURSES

Gail L. Schumann, University of Massachusetts
Patricia J. Vittum, University of Massachusetts
Monica L. Elliott, University of Florida
Patricia P. Cobb, Auburn University

JOHN WILEY & SONS, INC.

Library of Congress Cataloging-in-Publication Data:

IPM handbook for golf courses / Gail L. Schumann . . . [et al.].
   p. cm.
  Includes bibliographical references and index.
  ISBN 1-57504-065-4
  1. Golf courses—United States—Management—Handbooks, manuals, etc.
2. Pests—Control—United States—Handbooks, manuals, etc.
I. Schumann, Gail L. (Gail Lynn), 1951-
GV975.5.I75   1997
796.352'06'9—dc21   97-22730
                                CIP

Printed in the United States of America

10 9 8 7 6 5 4

ABOUT THE AUTHORS

Dr. Gail L. Schumann is Associate Professor of Plant Pathology at the University of Massachusetts at Amherst. She teaches courses in general plant pathology and turfgrass diseases, provides disease diagnostic services, and conducts research on turfgrass diseases.

Dr. Patricia J. Vittum is Associate Professor of Entomology at the University of Massachusetts at Amherst. She teaches courses in turfgrass entomology, greenhouse entomology, and pesticides in the environment. She is also the pesticide coordinator for pesticide education in Massachusetts and conducts research on turfgrass insects, including biology, biological control strategies, and pesticide application technology.

Dr. Monica L. Elliott is Associate Professor of Plant Pathology at the University of Florida's Fort Lauderdale Research and Education Center. She conducts research and maintains an active extension program on warm season turfgrasses, diseases, and general management. She has developed and worked with IPM programs since 1980.

Dr. Patricia P. Cobb is Professor, Extension Entomologist, at Auburn University, Alabama. She has primary extension responsibilities in turf and ornamentals entomology, and has developed and co-taught courses in landscape IPM and landscape entomology. Her research has focused on mapping, monitoring, and management of soil insect pests of turf, and on development of IPM strategies, including application technology.

INTRODUCTION

This book originated in a GCSAA-sponsored seminar, "Introduction to Integrated Pest Management," which was created by two of the authors, P.P. Cobb and P.J. Vittum, in 1989. Over the past seven years, different pairs of the four authors have been instructors for the seminar across the country. From this experience, the authors decided to summarize the basics of IPM in written form for golf course superintendents.

All of the authors have university faculty positions that include extension responsibilities. They enjoy this direct contact with the turfgrass industry, and all feel that they learn from innovative superintendents every year. To reflect these contributions, each chapter includes quotes from working superintendents. In addition, the final section presents portraits of IPM programs on golf courses from four different regions of the U.S.

A number of individuals generously contributed photographs, diagrams, and tables for this book. They have all been credited with their contributions. We wish to especially acknowledge Dr. Joseph Neal, North Carolina State University, for his review of the weed materials, and Dr. Robert Wick, University of Massachusetts, for his review of the nematode information.

TABLE OF CONTENTS

CHAPTER 1

INTRODUCTION

WHAT IS IPM?

IPM — What does this mean? These letters originally stood for "*Integrated Pest Management*," a concept which began in row crop agriculture.

The fundamental change in philosophy that accompanied this new concept was to shift from attempts to control pests—such as insects, pathogens, or weeds—with chemicals to using various strategies of management. We prefer to define IPM as *Intelligent Plant Management*.

After many years of intensive pesticide use, it is apparent that we will never be able to eliminate pests and pathogens because they are an integral part of the ecosystems in which they are found. This change is not quite as extreme as the old "if you can't lick 'em, join 'em" approach, but it does mean that we can learn to accept certain levels of injury and still have very acceptable playing conditions on the golf course. Instead of *crisis intervention*, management is a process that works *with the ecosystem* to take advantage of the natural checks and balances that help keep turf healthy and beautiful. This approach is less likely to result in destructive disruptions by disease and pest outbreaks.

Experienced golf course superintendents realize that the concept of IPM is not new. Every superintendent is, to some extent, practicing IPM already. IPM is a common sense process that continues to evolve over time. IPM never begins as a "complete" program. It generally begins with a few simple efforts and emerges over time as a complex, site-specific, and ever-changing program.

WHAT ARE THE BASICS?

Site Assessment

As a golf course (golfers, owners, and staff) makes a commitment to initiate an IPM program, it is absolutely crucial that the staff conduct an assessment of the golf course and the surrounding areas. This assessment should include maps indicating current irrigation and drainage, location of key trees, and soil types. In addition, it should include notation of the kinds of grasses being maintained, overall assessment of pest activity in recent years, and other maintenance items of interest. This step will

Figure 1.1. Sleepy Hollow Country Club, Scarborough, New York. (Courtesy P.J. Vittum.)

enable the golf course staff to document current conditions and to identify some of the areas which might be most vulnerable to pest activity. These are the areas which should be monitored most closely during the growing season. Site assessment is discussed in more detail in Chapter 2.

Monitoring

Another key component to any IPM program is routine (or regular) *monitoring,* or *scouting,* to determine what kinds of pests, diseases, or agronomic stresses might be present. Successful monitoring requires proper identification of pests and pathogens and knowledge of their life cycles or disease cycles (Figure 1.2). This information enables a golf course superintendent to determine when those pests will be most susceptible to management strategies.

Setting Thresholds

The concept of using *thresholds,* or *tolerance levels,* is another key to IPM, and is discussed in more detail in Chapter 3. During the scouting/monitoring process, insect counts, amount of disease-damaged turf, and number and types of weeds will be determined. Just because a scout finds insects feeding on the turf, or fungal activity on the greens, or weeds encroaching in the collars, does not mean that the superintendent will need to take immediate steps to manage the pest.

The decision to manage a pest and how to manage the pest will be determined by tolerance levels. These levels will vary for different portions of the course, different pests, and even different golf courses. For example, more weeds are tolerated in fairways than on putting greens. Tolerance levels are simply tools for making in-

Figure 1.2. Armyworms found in turf. How many is too many? (Courtesy P.P. Cobb.)

formed decisions. It is impossible to achieve perfection, so the superintendent and golfer *together* must determine tolerance levels or threshold levels.

Stress Management

A primary component of an IPM program is *stress management.* Many pests and pathogens cause little or no visible damage to turfgrass when the turf is actively growing and all the agronomic conditions (soil, water, drainage, mowing height, fertility) are nearly optimal. However, if some form of agronomic stress is present (too much water, too little water, low fertility, low mowing height, compaction), the same pest or pathogen may cause visible damage (Figure 1.3). Turf may be able to grow reasonably well and tolerate one or two stresses, but each additional stress threatens to result in unacceptable turf quality. Therefore, the backbone of an IPM program is a sound agronomic program that reduces plant stress.

Today's golf course superintendent was an environmentalist before it became the trend. We not only have a financial obligation to our employer to reduce pesticide use, but a moral obligation to the environment. Our main objective is to establish reasonable thresholds that will satisfy our golfing fraternity while demonstrating environmental responsibility. This can only be accomplished by identifying the most sensitive areas of our golf course and monitoring them. Scouting these hot spots will allow a responsible manager to be able to predict or anticipate a severe outbreak and apply materials as needed.

— Paul F. Miller, CGCS, Director of Golf Course Operations, Nashawtuc Country Club, Concord, Massachusetts

Figure 1.3. Turfgrass stressed on a slope where insect populations are highest. (Courtesy P.P. Cobb.)

Identifying and Optimizing Management Options

When a golf course superintendent has determined that a pest or pathogen is present at levels above the tolerance level for that part of the golf course, he or she must then consider the options available for managing the pest. Adjusting cultural management techniques may have a direct detrimental effect on the pest or may make the turf less attractive to the pest. There may be biological control agents available for use. However, in many cases, the most readily available option is to apply a chemical pesticide. Pesticides are *one* of the many tools used in an IPM program, but they must be selected and used very carefully.

In general, curative applications (made after a pest is already present) are easiest to apply in an IPM program for insect pests, and should be made only after monitoring has confirmed the presence of the insect. However, many fungicides (used for turf diseases) are most effective when applied *before* significant infection has occurred. This means that fungicides must be applied on a preventive basis for some diseases. Such an approach can still be justified in an IPM program, especially when all available cultural practices are in place. Fungicides may then be applied according to environmental prediction systems, rather than on a calendar basis, to avoid unnecessary use. Similarly, many herbicides must be applied before emergence of the target weed, but these materials can still be a valuable part of an IPM program. These concepts are discussed in more detail in Chapter 6.

Evaluation

The final concept that is invaluable in any IPM program is an evaluation of the results of the many components of the program. The *evaluation* will determine whether the approaches taken are maintaining pest damage to an acceptable level, whether timing of biological or chemical applications needs to be modified, and whether the costs are justified in terms of results. Evaluation is the step that determines how an IPM program will grow and evolve over time.

ADVANTAGES OF IPM

Economic: Instead of "spray and pray," IPM offers a cost-benefit analysis to determine the most economical approach to pest management.

Environmental: Overuse of pesticides can result in pest resistance and subsequent control failures, as well as non-target effects on other life forms in the turf ecosystem (Figure 1.4). IPM minimizes ecosystem disruption through an ecologically based management program. While there are exceptions, IPM programs often lead to an overall reduction in the amount of pesticides used during a growing season.

Public relations: Many members of the general public have inaccurate views of the environmental impact of golf courses. IPM plans document the complex array of science-based decisions to manage turfgrass pests and disease problems in an environmentally friendly manner.

Professionalism: An IPM plan is an organized approach to professional turfgrass management. It is essentially a contract between the superintendent, the crew, and the golfers about how decisions will be made and what results can be expected.

Figure 1.4. It is important to protect non-target life forms from overuse of pesticides. (Courtesy P.J. Vittum.)

PURPOSE OF THIS BOOK

This book is designed to offer a "field guide" approach to turfgrass IPM. It begins with general approaches to site assessment and monitoring for pests and diseases. It then describes the cultural, biological, and chemical strategies that may be included in an organized IPM plan. Specific management information for insect pests, diseases, and weeds follows. Some developing technologies with IPM potential are also described. Finally, some practical ideas on starting your own program are offered.

For beginners, we hope that this brief outline will encourage you to take advantage of the additional readings and educational programs you will need to understand the many complexities of modern turfgrass IPM. For more experienced turf managers who are already practicing IPM, we hope this handbook will give you new ideas for the continuing development of your program.

FURTHER READING

Baxendale, F.P. and R.E. Gaussoin, Eds. *Integrated Turfgrass Management for the Northern Great Plains.* Cooperative Extension, Institute of Agriculture and Natural Resources, University of Nebraska, Lincoln, NE, 1997.

Beard, J.B. The Benefits of Golf Course Turf. *Golf Course Management,* 64(3):57–61, 1996.

Bruneau, A.A., D.J. Watkins, and R.L. Brandenburg. Integrated Pest Management, in *Turfgrass, Agronomy Monograph 32*, Waddington, D.V., R.N. Carrow, and R.C. Shearman, Eds., ASA, CSSA, and SSSA, Madison, WI, 1992.

Fermanian, T.W., M.C. Shurtleff, R. Randell, H.T. Wilkinson, and P.L. Nixon. *Controlling Turfgrass Pests.* Prentice-Hall, Inc., Upper Saddle River, NJ, 1997.

Karnok, K.J., Ed. *Turfgrass Management Information Directory.* Ann Arbor Press, Chelsea, MI, 1996.

Leslie, A.R., Ed. *Handbook of Integrated Pest Management for Turf and Ornamentals*, Lewis Publishers, Boca Raton, FL, 1994.

McCarty, B. Best Management Practices for Golf Courses. *Golf Course Management,* 64(4):55–57, 1995.

Watschke, T.L., P.H. Dernoeden, and D. Shetlar. *Managing Turfgrass Pests.* Lewis Publishers, Boca Raton, FL, 1995.

CHAPTER 2

SITE ASSESSMENT

An important first step in establishing an IPM program is to assess your current resources and the condition of the IPM site and surrounding areas. Site assessment is important whether a golf course is still on the drawing board or has existed for decades. This chapter discusses the information you need to develop landscape and golf course profiles, pest profiles, how to make use of native vegetation, and how to optimize your current management practices.

GOLF COURSE PROFILES

Golf course profiles, or maps, are useful for keeping records of conditions and changes at a site. These maps include the golf course turf and the surrounding landscape.

Important information to record and map includes:

- Drainage patterns; drainage lines
- Irrigation system
- Soil texture
- Elevation variations
- Shade patterns, including seasonal variations
- Traffic patterns
- Location of strategic native plants and landscaped areas
- Surface waters: streams, ponds
- Historical areas of insect, nematode, and disease injury and weed infestations
- Past notes from scouting/monitoring records
- Areas where pest and agronomic problems recur
- Areas for potential renovation or alteration

Site profiles/maps can be made from:

- Scorecards as outlines for individual hand drawings of each hole (roughs and surrounding nonmanaged areas can be added) (Figure 2.2)
- Irrigation or property blueprints (Figure 2.3)
- Aerial photographs

Figure 2.1. Rocks placed in turf drainage area to aid drainage and reduce erosion. (Courtesy P.P. Cobb.)

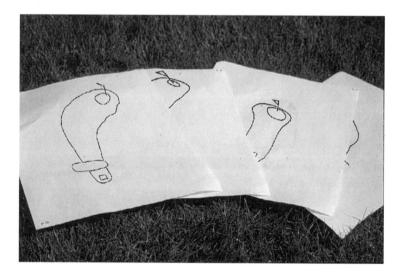

Figure 2.2. Maps used for mapping of mole cricket infestations made from score cards. (Courtesy P.P. Cobb.)

- Computer-generated maps (Figure 2.4)
- Global positioning systems (Figure 2.5)

Draw in landmarks:

- Trees and shrubs
- 150-yard markers
- Sprinkler heads

- Greens
- Tees
- Bunkers

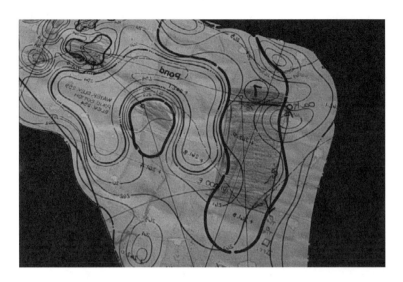

Figure 2.3. Map of mole cricket infestations made from golf course blueprints. Tawny mole cricket females lay eggs in areas where they are active in late winter and/or early spring. Map early-season areas of activity and treat only these areas at a time when pest susceptibility is greatest for a particular control product or activity. (Courtesy P.P. Cobb.)

Why map pest problem areas?

- To identify infested areas for treatment: Treating only infested areas reduces application costs by limiting use of control products to these areas only. It also reduces human and environmental exposure to pesticides.
- To determine when areas become reinfested over time: Soil insect pests may prefer slopes with southern exposures in the northern hemisphere. Recurring weed problems may be linked to drainage patterns.
- To help identify pest "reservoirs" in roughs and surrounding areas.
- To facilitate good communication with club officials, golfers, and public by documenting pest problem areas.

Changes in Golf Course Profiles

Once a profile has been created, copies should be generated to record changes, both major and minor, to maintain up-to-date records of each site.

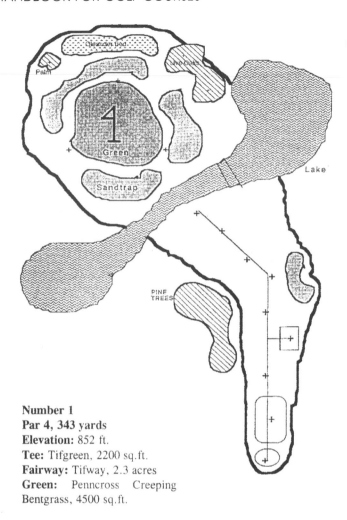

Number 1
Par 4, 343 yards
Elevation: 852 ft.
Tee: Tifgreen, 2200 sq.ft.
Fairway: Tifway, 2.3 acres
Green: Penncross Creeping
Bentgrass, 4500 sq.ft.

Figure 2.4. Computer-drawn map of Tiger Golf Course. (Courtesy L.B. McCarty.)

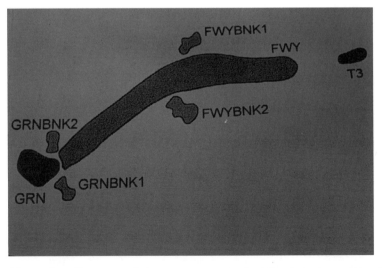

Figure 2.5. Map of golf course fairway generated with global positioning system (GPS). (Courtesy D. Reynolds.)

PEST PROFILES

Pest profiles are a summary of important information that you want easily available when problems occur. These should be developed for each insect pest, disease problem, and weed that you expect to manage on your golf course. An example of each is given. Modify the categories of information as needed for your conditions.

A sample outline might include:

Pest
> Common name and scientific (Latin) name

Symptoms
> What to watch for in turf when this pest is active

Favorable Environmental Conditions
> Seasonal and weather conditions that favor pest activity

Biology
> How to identify the pest or pathogen
> General life cycle
> When and how damage occurs
> Where pest is found
> Which stages are susceptible to management

Scouting/Monitoring
> Best monitoring techniques
> Tolerance or threshold levels
> Predictive models, if any

Cultural Control Practices
> Conditions that favor pest (for example: excess thatch, fertility imbalance)
> Practices that may make turf less favorable for pest (for example: raise mowing height temporarily, irrigate at midday)

Biological Control Options
> Commercial products
> Timing of application
> Special conditions (shelf life, application methods)

Chemical Control Options
> Pre- or post-application irrigation
> Groundwater concerns
> How quickly a product works
> How long a product lasts
> Reliability
> Effects on non-target organisms

References
> Extension publications
> Texts
> Trade magazine articles

Figure 2.6. Annual bluegrass weevil damage. See Color Plate 1. (Courtesy P.J. Vittum.)

INSECT PEST PROFILE EXAMPLE: Annual Bluegrass Weevil (Hyperodes weevil)

Common and Latin Names: Annual Bluegrass Weevil, *Listronotus maculicollis*

This small weevil attacks annual bluegrass that is maintained at relatively low mowing heights. It is most damaging in the metropolitan New York area and normally completes two or three generations per year.

Symptoms

The insect attacks annual bluegrass, particularly that which is mowed at or below 0.75 inches (2 cm). Affected areas begin as small, irregular yellow patches which gradually coalesce. When damage becomes severe, patches appear water-soaked. Damage first becomes apparent in late spring or early summer, normally along the edges of fairways or on collars bordering woods. The second generation moves farther into the golf course, and may cause damage on any low-cut annual bluegrass.

Favorable Environmental Conditions

Mild winters or winters with substantial periods of snow cover seem to favor weevil survival, and therefore result in higher initial populations in the spring. Large numbers of eastern white pines (*Pinus strobus*) in neighboring woods also provide excellent protection for winter survival. Golf courses with large areas of annual bluegrass provide ideal conditions for the insect to thrive. The insect appears to be active in a wide range of soil types, but adequate soil and thatch moisture appear to be critical to survival.

Life Cycle

Adults winter in leaf litter under white pines or other trees or woods near golf courses. In the spring they migrate to the fairways and lower-cut areas of the golf course, where females lay *eggs* inside leaf sheaths. The eggs hatch into tiny legless *larvae* (cream-colored with brown heads) (Figure 2.7) which begin to feed inside the stem. Within a week, they become too large to remain inside the plant, and emerge to feed near the base of the plant. They complete five larval stages in about a month. They then move down into the upper part of the root zone and *pupate* for about a week. Young *adults* emerge and move actively on the turf surface for about a week before mating and producing a *second generation*.

Cycles in the metropolitan New York area are:

First generation:

egg laying	late April or early May
large larvae	early to mid June
pupae	late June
young adults	late June or early July

Second generation:

eggs	mid to late July
large larvae	early to mid August
overwintering adults	September

In warm years, each step occurs earlier in the year, and there is a third generation in late summer.

Scouting/Monitoring

Larvae: (Active in thatch)

1. Cut a wedge of turf with a knife and visually inspect the sample for larvae and pupae.

   – or –

2. Cut a cup-cutter plug, gently tease the turf apart, and visually inspect the thatch (and upper root zone) for larvae and pupae. After completing the inspection, place the sample in a container, fill it with warm water, and check the surface of the water after about 5 minutes. Any larvae or pupae missed in the initial inspection will float to the surface.

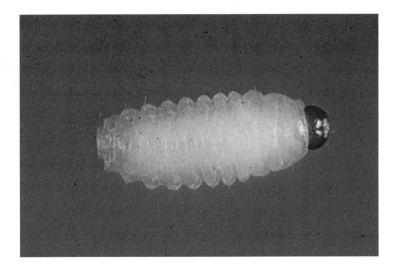

Figure 2.7. Annual bluegrass weevil larva. See Color Plate 2. (Courtesy New York State Turfgrass Association.)

Adults: (Active on the turfgrass surface, especially on sunny days, and in the thatch)

1. Get down on hands and knees and watch for insects moving across the surface. Concentrate on areas where the height of cut changes, and around small holes or scars.

   – or –

2. Use a soapy flush (irritating drench) to force adults to the surface.

Threshold Levels:

Vary from 30 to 80 larvae per square foot in spring to as low as 10 to 40 larvae per square foot in summer.

Cultural Control Practices to Reduce Insect Activity

Reduce the amount of annual bluegrass.

- Renovate where appropriate, replacing with bentgrasses or ryegrasses.
- Use plant growth regulators to put annual bluegrass at a competitive disadvantage with desirable turf species.
- Reduce spring irrigation to encourage deeper rooting of bentgrasses and enhance their summer survival.

Raise the mowing height.

- Insect activity appears to be most severe at lower heights of cut.

Remove white pine litter in autumn or spring.

- Adult weevils spend the winter in pine litter, so removal should reduce overwintering populations.

Biological Control Options to Reduce Insect Development and Damage

Entomopathogenic Nematodes

Natural populations of *Steinernema carpocapsae* have been observed suppressing annual bluegrass weevil larval populations. However, field trials of commercial formulations of this nematode have not been conclusive.

Parasitic Braconid Wasp

Microctonus hyperodae has been providing excellent suppression of a very closely related weevil in New Zealand pastures. Further studies are needed to determine whether that wasp or another wasp, *Microtonus aethiopoides,* can be effective against the annual bluegrass weevil in the United States.

Chemical Control Options to Reduce Insect Development and Damage

Insecticide Options

To reduce insecticide use, a perimeter treatment on fairways, greens, and tees may be sufficient in the spring. Larger areas are treated in the summer.

- organophosphates: chlorpyrifos, isazofos, isofenphos, trichlorfon

Adequate population reduction is achieved fairly consistently.

- carbamates: bendiocarb
- synthetic pyrethroids: bifenthrin, cyfluthrin, cyhalothrin

Several are being tested and some seem to provide reasonable levels of control.

Tank Mixes

Combinations of a pyrethroid and another product sometimes seem to enhance the performance, perhaps because the pyrethroid irritates the weevils so that they are more active and come in contact with more insecticide.

Label Restrictions

The annual bluegrass weevil is not currently included on the label of some of these products, so follow label directions and check local regulations before using any product.

Timing

Application timing is critical. Most spring applications should be made shortly after forsythia is in full bloom and shortly before flowering dogwood (*Cornus florida*) is in full bloom. Most summer applications should be made within a week of July 4th in the metropolitan New York area. Timing varies depending on spring temperatures.

Figure 2.8. Symptoms of brown patch on colonial bentgrass. See Color Plate 4. (Courtesy G.L. Schumann.)

DISEASE PEST PROFILE EXAMPLE: Brown Patch (Rhizoctonia Blight)

Disease and Pathogen: Brown Patch, *Rhizoctonia solani*

This fungus survives all year in soil and thatch and is present in abundance in nearly every turfgrass area. Different genetic strains of the fungus are involved in the disease. Because of these pathogen variations, the disease varies in both symptoms and favorable environmental conditions in different regions and on different turfgrass species.

Symptoms

While individual leaf symptoms vary with the grass species, the overall effect is a circular patch (small or large) of blighted turfgrass.

Creeping bentgrass at putting green height:

Patches of blighted turf, often with a grayish "smoke ring" observed at the leading edge of the patch during periods of high relative humidity.

Other cool-season grasses at higher mowing heights:

Perennial ryegrass and tall fescue are particularly susceptible. Relatively large blighted patches, often with no smoke ring; lesions on individual leaf blades, usually irregular with a dark border.

Warm-season turfgrasses:

Large patches usually without smoke ring or leaf lesions; basal rot of leaves; leaves can be easily pulled from leaf sheaths.

Favorable Environmental Conditions Required for Disease Development

Relative Humidity: > 95% (= leaf wetness) for 10 hr or more
Soil Temperatures: mean > 70°F (21°C); minimum > 64°F (18°C)
Air Temperatures: mean > 68°F (20°C); minimum > 59°F (15°C)
Rainfall/Irrigation: 0.1 inches (3 mm) received in the 36 hr preceding the tenth hour of high relative humidity

Temperatures apply to the 24 hr preceding the 10th hour of high relative humidity. Disease can also occur at somewhat lower air temperatures following heavy rainfall and extended hours of leaf wetness.

If temperature falls below 59°F (15°C) in the 48 hr following the environmental conditions necessary for disease development, no disease will occur.

These conditions may be used for disease prediction to help with timing of fungicides in many areas of the northeastern United States.

Disease/Pathogen Cycle

Cool-season turfgrasses:

The fungus is most active in the summer months during hot, humid weather with extended dew, rainfall, and warm night temperatures.

The fungus survives the rest of the year as sclerotia and mycelia in plant debris.

Warm-season turfgrasses:

The fungus is most active in spring and fall months, and in southern Florida in winter. Disease is not observed in southern areas in summer because temperatures are too high for this subgroup of *R. solani* and ideal for growing turfgrass. The fungus survives during these periods as sclerotia and mycelia in plant debris.

Cultural Control Practices to Reduce Disease Development and Damage

Fertilization:

Moderate nitrogen fertilization during disease-conducive weather. Disease is more likely to occur when excessive N fertilizer, especially quick-release N sources, is applied.

Reduce Leaf Wetness:

Drag or mow dew from turf surface. Time irrigation to favor rapid drying of leaf blades. Modify landscaping and other practices to increase air movement.

Thatch Management:

Reduce thatch to reduce potential pathogen populations. Thatch is one place the fungus lies dormant until favorable environmental conditions for disease development occur.

Biological Control Options to Reduce Disease Development and Damage

Biological control agents have recently been registered for turfgrass diseases. Commercial examples include:

BioTrek 22G (Wilbur Ellis Co.) — a granular formulation of the fungus
  Trichoderma harzianum
BioJect (EcoSoils Systems) — a strain of the bacterium *Pseudomonas
  aureofaceans*

There are limited field data concerning the successful use of these very new products in commercial turfgrass sites.

Researchers have achieved control of brown patch in experimental field plots with the following fungi:

Gliocladium (Trichoderma) virens   Binucleate *Rhizoctonia* spp.

Certain compost materials have been shown to suppress brown patch, but these materials should be used with caution. You need to experiment with them on your course and should probably not expect to use them as your sole source of disease control. (See Chapter 7.)

Chemical Control Options to Reduce Disease Development and Damage

Predictive models have been published to aid in the timing of fungicide applications. One of the models is available in commercial weather stations. (See Chapter 11.) The disease prediction model may not reduce fungicide applications, but it should improve fungicide efficacy. To reduce fungicide use, use past disease records and apply fungicides preventively only to those areas with a history of brown patch.

Contact Fungicides: chlorothalonil, mancozeb, maneb, thiram, PCNB. Follow label directions for rates and application intervals.

Localized Penetrant Fungicides: iprodione, vinclozolin. Follow label directions for rates and application intervals.

Acropetal (upward-moving) Penetrant Fungicides: azoxystrobin, cyproconazole, fenarimol, flutolanil, myclobutanil, propiconazole, triadimefon, thiophanate-methyl. Follow label directions for rates and application intervals.

It is important to read fungicide labels completely. Some fungicides are only useful as preventive materials for brown patch. They must be tank-mixed with other fungicides if brown patch is already active.

Figure 2.9. Dandelion. (Courtesy J. Bresnahan.)

WEED PEST PROFILE EXAMPLE: Dandelion

Common and Latin Names: Dandelion, *Taraxacum officinale*

[Common names of plants sometimes vary by geographic region, so it can be helpful to also note the Latin name to avoid confusion in written information and herbicide labels.]

Identification

Dandelion is a common perennial, broadleaf weed in turfgrass. The plant forms a rosette of long, narrow, deeply lobed leaves. The flower is bright yellow and quickly produces numerous wind-disseminated seeds. The plant has a large, fleshy taproot that can penetrate deeply into soil, making removal difficult.

Cultural Control Options to Reduce Weed Infestation

- As with most weeds, a dense, competitive turfgrass is the best strategy to minimize weed encroachment. Appropriate fertilizer applications and insect and disease management are important.
- Physical removal is effective when the number of plants is small.

Biological Control Options to Reduce Weed Infestation

No commercial biocontrol agents for turfgrass weeds are yet available, but research has been conducted on pests and pathogens with potential for biological management. These have particular potential in turfgrass, where a weed weakened by a disease may be more easily crowded out by turfgrass plants.

Chemical Control Options to Reduce Weed Infestations

- Selective, broadleaf, post-emergence herbicides are commonly used.
  Examples: mixture of 2,4-D, mecoprop, and dicamba
  mixture of 2,4-D and triclopyr
- Fall applications are most effective.
- Spot applications can be effective for dandelions because individual plants are obvious.

USE OF NATIVE PLANTS

Golf course turfgrass is normally a highly maintained landscape requiring frequent mowing. It is often composed of one or a few species of relatively uniform plants, which makes it vulnerable to disease and insect problems. Highly maintained turfgrass areas can be minimized and replaced by use of native vegetation or plants well-adapted to your specific environment, including other turfgrass species (Figures 2.10 through 2.12).

> When I came to this course as a first-time superintendent (1986), the golf course had been farmland. I knew it wasn't going to be a high-budget operation. There were no trees. In spite of frustration, I decided to stay.
>
> My first challenge was to establish trees and shrubs on the golf course. I developed a 5-year tree-planting plan that was cost-effective

Figure 2.10. Use of native grasses around a tee reduces mowing in the tee area. Collier's Reserve Golf Course, Naples, Florida. (Courtesy P.P. Cobb.)

Figure 2.11. #10 Fairway in winter before planting with native trees. (Courtesy P.P. Cobb.)

Figure 2.12. #10 Fairway 10 years after planting with native trees. Red Eagle Golf Course, Eufaula, Alabama. (Courtesy P.P. Cobb.)

in materials and labor. Most trees and shrubs were dug from surrounding wooded areas and planted during the winter season.

Overall, these trees have been more drought and cold tolerant and have been more insect and disease resistant than those purchased from nurseries. These native plants have improved the course landscape and "playability." On a tight budget, this plan has continued to be affordable.

— Neil Yarbrough, Golf Course Superintendent, Red Eagle Golf Course, Eufaula, Alabama

Maintenance Advantages

- Reduced maintenance costs
- Reduced maintenance problems on steep and isolated areas that are difficult to mow
- Reduced potential need for pesticide applications to turfgrass areas
- Reduced water and fertilizer inputs in natural areas
- Reduced area requiring intensive IPM scouting and monitoring

Ecological Advantages

- Increased diversity in wildlife habitats can increase both numbers of species and total numbers of wildlife.
- Increased beauty and variety of non-turf landscape areas.
- Natural areas can serve as "buffer zones" between highly maintained turfgrass and environmentally sensitive areas such as streams and marshes.

Cautions

- Do not allow natural areas to interfere with light penetration and air circulation on turfgrass areas. This may increase disease problems.
- In some cases, planting of non-native plants that are well-adapted to your environment will be more easily maintained or visually appealing than restoration of native vegetation. Take care to choose plants that will grow successfully in your hardiness zone, and anticipate how they will look as part of a mature landscape.
- Natural areas may still require considerable planning and labor to be established.
- Natural areas may require maintenance, such as annual mowing, to maintain their appearance and variety.

> For natural areas, start small, educate, and expand with a relationship to acceptance. We began with stream, river, and pond bank naturalization, and have now expanded to non-use course areas.
>
> — Michael Gunn, Golf Course Superintendent, Wahconah Country Club, Dalton, Massachusetts

BUILDING ON YOUR EXISTING PROGRAM

Before moving into specific methods and plans, it can be useful to evaluate your current situation. Past records are the key to future planning. The following information will be useful for frequent consultation:

- Landscape and golf course profiles
- Pest profiles for all potential problems in your area:
  - Insect pests
  - Diseases
  - Weeds
- Past expense records for pest management
- Past problems that have been difficult to prevent or correct
- Past problems that have elicited the most complaints from the golfers (i.e., use of particular pesticides or injury from specific pests)
- Areas for renovation with improved turfgrass cultivars and species
- Areas for potential conversion from turfgrass to other vegetation
- Areas where IPM practices are likely to make the most difference (i.e., where injury tolerance is higher and problems have been recurring)
- Areas where management is likely to continue to require intense preventive management in the near future (i.e., putting greens, fairways near the clubhouse)
- Areas where experiments can be conducted to determine the relative costs, benefits, and risks associated with various practices (i.e., nontreated areas, spot treatments, different pesticide rates, products, or tank mixes can be tested in a scientifically sound manner) (Figure 2.13). These may best be conducted in more out-of-the-way areas, the turf nursery, or, in some cases, in an area where you can showcase your efforts to improve practices.

Figure 2.13. Split fairway test for mole cricket control. Left: not treated; right: treated. (Courtesy P.P. Cobb.)

FURTHER READING

Burpee, L.L. A Method for Assessing the Efficacy of a Biocontrol Agent on Dandelion (*Taraxacum officinale*). *Weed Technol.* 6:401–403, 1992.

Christian, N. Developing a Testing Program on the Golf Course. *Golf Course Management.* 58(12):32–40, 1990.

Ciekot, D. Native and Naturalized. *Golf Course Management.* 64(3):100–108, 1996.

Cigard, J.F. X-scape from the Ordinary. *Golf Course Management.* 63(11):20–32, 1995.

Fech, J.C. and D.H. Steinegger. Ornamental Grasses. *Golf Course Management.* 64(4):56–60, 1996.

Harker, D., S. Evans, M. Evans, and K. Harker. *Landscape Restoration Handbook.* Lewis Publishers, Boca Raton, FL, 1993.

Hartwiger, C.E. Landscape Naturalization in Turfgrass Management. *Golf Course Management.* 63(9):58–59, 1995.

Riddle, G.E., L.L. Burpee, and G.J. Boland. Virulence of *Sclerotinia sclerotiorum* and *S. minor* on Dandelion (*Taraxacum officinale*). *Weed Sci.* 39:109–118, 1991.

CHAPTER **3**

SCOUTING AND MONITORING

One of the cornerstones of any IPM program is *scouting* or *monitoring* the golf course on a regular basis. Scouting enables the golf course superintendent to monitor pest presence and development throughout the growing season. By observing turf conditions regularly (daily, weekly, or monthly, depending on the pest) and noting which pests are present, a superintendent can make intelligent decisions regarding possible pest control strategies. At the same time, scouting enables the superintendent to monitor agronomic and other cultural developments (or stresses) in the turf and to recognize patterns on the golf course. It is essential to *record* the results of scouting and monitoring in order to develop historical information, document patterns of pest activity, and document successes (and failures) of control activities (Tables 3.1 and 3.2).

WHAT TO LOOK FOR

What does the damage look like?

- Are there several discrete patches, each a similar size and appearance?
- How large are the patches?
- Do they coalesce (become larger until they form one large patch)?
- What color are the patches?
- Do the individual leaf blades have lesions?
- Is the turf intact or is it torn up in some fashion?
- Can the affected turf be pulled up easily?
- Are weeds present?

Where does the damage occur?

- Is the damage occurring on all of the grasses present or only on one species or cultivar?
- Is the entire area affected or is the damage concentrated in certain areas?
  - shady areas? (Figure 3.3)
  - edges of fairways?
  - south-facing slopes? (Figure 3.4)
  - poorly drained areas?
  - greens with little or no air circulation?
  - sandy soils?
  - particular species or cultivars of turfgrass?

Table 3.1. Example of field history report form used for golf courses. (Courtesy L.B. McCarty.)

Turf IPM Field History Report Form

Club _____ Superintendent _____ Date _____

Hole Number _____ Scout _____ Phone Number _____

Phone Number _____

Site	Turf Species	Area	Mowing Schedule	Soil Analysis pH	Soil Analysis P	Soil Analysis K	Soil Drainage	Fertilization Amount (N/1000 ft²) Spring	Summer	Fall	Winter	Frequency	Irrigation Scheduling
Green													
Tee													
Fairway													
Rough													
Driving Range													
Nursery Green													
Practice Green													

Comments on specific topics, such as shade, overseeding blend, nitrogen carrier, top-dressing mix, weather, irrigation salinity levels, etc.:

_____

_____

_____

Table 3.2. Example of field infestation report form used for southern golf courses. (Courtesy L.B. McCarty.)

Field Infestation Report Form

Club _____   Superintendent _____   Phone Number _____   Date _____

Hole Number _____   Scout _____   Phone Number _____

Site	Turf Species	Mowing Height	Soil Moisture	Weeds Species/No. or %	Diseases Species/No. or %	Insects Species/No. or %	Nematodes Species/No. or %
Green							
Tee							
Fairway							
Rough							

Notes:

Weeds
1. Goosegrass
2. Crabgrass
3. Dallisgrass/ Thin Paspalum
4. Torpedograss
5. Broadleaves
6. Nutsedge (Yellow, Globe, Purple, Annual, Kyllinga)
7. *Poa annua*
8. Kikuyugrass
9. Other

Diseases
1. Dollar Spot
2. Leaf Spot
3. *Pythium* Blight
4. *Pythium* Root Rot
5. Fairy Ring
6. Brown Patch (*R. solani*)
7. Rhizoctonia Leaf and Sheath Blight (*R. zeae*)
8. Bermudagrass Decline
9. Snow Mold
10. Red Thread
11. Algae/Moss
12. Other

Insects
1. Mole Crickets
2. Sod Webworms
3. Armyworms
4. Cutworms
5. White Grubs
6. Fire Ants
7. Mites
8. Grass Scales
9. Other

Nematodes
1. Sting
2. Lance
3. Stubby-Root
4. Root-Knot
5. Cyst
6. Ring
7. Spiral
8. Sheath
9. Other

Figure 3.1. IPM scout at work. (Courtesy P.P. Cobb.)

Figure 3.2. IPM scout at work. (Courtesy P.P. Cobb.)

When does the damage occur?

Most turf damage that is caused by living organisms occurs at roughly the same time each growing season. Note when the damage is observed and note any trees or shrubs that may be flowering (or just leafing out or showing some other notable stage of development) at the same time (Figure 3.5). This can provide a point of comparison in subsequent years.

Figure 3.3. Heavily shaded green can result in development of algae (or moss). (Courtesy M.L. Elliott.)

Figure 3.4. Mole cricket damage on a slope. Soil insect pest infestations begin in the spring on slope exposures where sun is most intense. Southern slopes in the northern hemisphere may be where these pests first infest new golf courses. (Courtesy P.P. Cobb.)

What abiotic (environmental) conditions are present at the time of damage?

- What are the conditions of soil texture, moisture, and temperature?
- Is there soil compaction (often related to traffic patterns)?
- What are the conditions of thatch moisture, thickness, and density?
- How is the drainage?

Figure 3.5. Lilac (*Syringa*) bloom and other stages of plant development may be useful for initiating monitoring for certain pest problems. (Courtesy F.D. Dinelli.)

- What are the irrigation patterns?
  - localized dry spots?
  - inadequate overlap?
  - leaky heads?
- How is the air circulation?
  - too many trees and shrubs surrounding a green?
- How many hours of direct sunlight or shade are there?
- What is the direction and degree of slope?
- What is the mowing height and frequency?
- Does the damage occur during or following a certain kind of weather?
  - high night temperatures?
  - high humidity?
  - heavy rainfall?
- What are the fertility levels, especially nitrogen?

Diseases: In New England (The Berkshires), dollar spot is our worst disease. Keeping a close eye on fertilizer levels, temperature variation, and the weather forecasts is key to whether I spray preventively or curatively. This is just a practical form of IPM.

Strong cultural practices are the backbone of growing quality turf. As a superintendent, I've practiced that all my life, as most superintendents do. I guess we've been on the cutting edge of IPM for a long time.

Scouting and Monitoring: I can remember when I first started. An older superintendent took me out early one morning to scout. He told me, "I look for bird activity in the fairways. When I see higher than normal amounts, I start digging around looking for grubs." What a great monitoring tool!

I think all superintendents use IPM. It can be as simple as the guy who picks broadleaf weeds out of his greens with a jackknife to the superintendent who uses infrared imagery to locate stresses on turf caused by insects.

— Bruce Packard, CGCS, Stockbridge Golf Club, Stockbridge, Massachusetts

ESTABLISHING THRESHOLDS

Insect, disease, or weed pests that occur on golf courses cannot be completely eliminated, so golf course superintendents must learn to manage their turfgrass in the presence of these pests. At the same time, turfgrass usually can tolerate one or two sources of stress without visible effects. When several stresses occur at the same time, however, the turf begins to suffer visibly.

One key aspect of an IPM program is determining what the tolerance level is for each pest. In row crop agriculture, the term *economic threshold* is used to identify the point at which the cost of the loss in yield from pest pressure is greater than the cost of applying a control strategy. Since one does not measure "yield" in determining the value of a golf course, it is impossible to make the same kinds of economic analyses. Turf IPM programs normally determine *tolerance levels* or *aesthetic thresholds*. In other words, how many white grubs — or dollar spots or crabgrass plants — are too many?

Tolerance levels on a golf course will be very site-specific and will depend on several things:

- Pest species present or combination of pests present
- Turfgrass species and cultivar and its inherent tolerance to the pest
- Turf use (green vs. tee vs. fairway vs. rough)
- Vigor and condition of turf
  - availability of water
  - drainage
  - mowing height and frequency
  - nutritional level
- Time of year (ability of turf to recuperate from damage; rate of pest increase)
- Expectations of the golfers
- Tournament schedule

- Availability of curative control options (if there is no control option which will work after a pest becomes established, decisions to treat or not treat must be made sooner)
- Budget considerations

> Course setup is done every day and always by an assistant or turf student who acts as the scout and reports back to the superintendent.
>
> In 1996, we did *not* spray for *Pythium* at all. In the past five seasons, we have sprayed for *Pythium* four times, and only once did we do a complete spray.
>
> Reducing our water pH has greatly enhanced the effect and longevity of our chemicals.
>
> — Joseph Alonzi, CGCS, Westchester Country Club, Rye, New York

SETTING PRIORITIES, DEFINING PATTERNS

Scouts normally will not have time to scout every inch of the property every day, so priorities must be established. In many cases a golf course IPM program will start by including a small portion of the course and gradually expand as expertise and confidence build.

Frequency of monitoring should be greater:

- For greens than for fairways, and least for roughs
- When recuperative potential of turf is poor
- When a pest is present or expected
- When weather conditions account for added stress (high or low temperatures, high or low rainfall)
- When a tournament is scheduled

Patterns for mapping vary with the pest, golf course layout, and personal preferences. The primary objective is to produce a reasonably thorough map of the golf course which shows where the pest activity is greatest or where agronomic conditions may be accounting for stress or disease, and then to begin to determine why those areas are infested or affected.

Mapping options include:

- Grid patterns
  (Make observations every 20 to 30 yards (meters) along a fairway or rough, with 10 to 15 yards (meters) separating each series of observations.)
- Zigzag patterns
- A series of transect lines

MONITORING FOR EVALUATION

If a management strategy (whether a traditional pesticide, a biocontrol agent, or a cultural practice modification) is used to reduce a pest or disease problem, there is no way of knowing whether that practice was effective unless the area is sampled *before and after* treatment. This aspect of monitoring is often overlooked. However, it is a very important part of an IPM program because it documents the effectiveness of the practice and helps determine whether the cost and effort resulted in the desired outcome.

Some important components of evaluation include:

- Determine if the management practice reduced the pest population (i.e., compare pre-treatment counts with post-treatment counts).
- If the condition did improve, make notes about factors that may have contributed to the successful action (e.g., weather conditions, irrigation, time of day).
- If the condition did not improve, try to determine why the management strategy failed (e.g., unexpected weather conditions, water pH, time of day, inappropriate or wrong pesticide, inactive biological control agent, improper watering before or after the action was taken).

SEASONAL CHANGES IN PEST ACTIVITY

Do not scout for a pest during times when the pest is not likely to be found. For example, white grubs will be present in cool-season grasses in early spring and again from late summer through the autumn. Do not look for those grubs in late spring or early summer. Similarly, some weeds do not germinate until summer. Do not look for them in the spring.

CAN YOU JUSTIFY THE COST OF A SCOUT?

A cost-benefit analysis of scouting may help you to determine if the additional cost is justified.

Benefits

- Better records
  (pest activity, local phenology, turf conditions, weather data)
- Document presence or absence of pests
  (helps justify pesticide use and satisfy some federal, state, or local regulations)
- Improve your understanding of the dynamics of the golf course

(effects of weather on pests, locations and possible explanations for "hot spots," comparisons from one year to another)
- *May* reduce pesticide use with some confidence
(spot treatments in identified hot spots, optimized timing of applications, extended interval between applications)
- Public relations
(enhance professional image with golfers, as well as local and state officials)

Costs

- Cost of labor (time spent scouting)
- Risk of misdiagnosis, especially when still learning to identify some pests
- Risk of obtaining a diagnosis too late to apply a curative control
- Initial loss of peace of mind
(fewer pesticide applications made for "insurance")
- *May* increase pesticide use
(identify pests that previously went unnoticed)

USING HISTORICAL INFORMATION

Insect, disease, or weed pests tend to recur in the same areas from one year to another, as long as growing conditions are comparable. If accurate records are kept each year, noting *where* pest activity occurs, *when* it occurs, and what trees and shrubs are blooming (or leaf out) at the same time, a superintendent can learn to anticipate pest activity in particular locations and concentrate on monitoring those areas before the pests become established.

> *Example:* The annual bluegrass weevil typically attacks annual bluegrass on the edges of fairways (and collars) in late spring, about four weeks after dogwoods are in full bloom. A superintendent can make note of areas with damage in previous years and begin monitoring those areas about two weeks after dogwood is in full bloom. Small larvae can be seen in the thatch before the annual bluegrass goes "off color" in early summer.

TRAINING SCOUTS

Golf course superintendents often designate one or two employees to be responsible for monitoring the golf course on a regular basis. These individuals will couple their scouting responsibilities with other duties, such as changing cups or perhaps being the spray technician. The importance of looking for pests and confirming their presence is critical. Just as critical is the communication *between* the scout(s) and the golf course superintendent.

Qualities to look for in an IPM scout

- Basic educational background in turf management or horticulture
- Understands the basic concepts and goals of IPM
- Observant
- Self-motivated
- Dependable
- Organized
- Communicates well orally and in writing

Primary objectives of a scout

- Identify target pests and potential secondary pests.
  (what? how many? where? when? growth stage?)
- Identify natural enemies.
  (what? how many? are there enough to reduce pest population adequately?)
- Locate "hot spots" where pest population is highest and most likely to cause visible damage.
- Identify maintenance activities that may affect pest activity.
  (mowing height, frequency or timing of irrigation, traffic patterns, fertilizer applications)
- Note weather conditions (daily and seasonal), such as:
  - air temperature (daily maximum and minimum)
  - soil temperature (and time of day when recorded)
  - precipitation and cloud cover
  - wind direction and speed
- May assist in developing thresholds.
- Communicate scouting results to superintendent.
- Evaluate results of actions taken.
  If a control measure is to be taken, obtain an estimate of the pest population *before* the control strategy is implemented, and then sample at a suitable interval after control. Did it work? If so, why? If not, why not?

Learning to Identify Pests

Begin to build a library of references, including trade magazines, state turf pest recommendations, textbooks, and identification guides. (See the lists provided in Appendix 1.) Most states have an active Cooperative Extension program with county, regional, or state specialists who have expertise in identification of pests and who conduct training programs to teach turf managers some of the identification basics. Arrange to send your designated scout to as many training programs as possible.

Provide the scout with the basic tools necessary to carry out the monitoring, including:

- sharp knife
- soil thermometer
- cup cutter
- hand trowel
- dish detergent
- hand lens (10–20x)
- pest and disease guides
- soil probe
- clipboard and recording forms
- "min-max" thermometer
- shovel or spade
- bucket
- rating grid
- plastic bags and bottles and identification tags

Access to a dissecting microscope is invaluable for identification of many insect pests, turfgrasses, and weeds, and some diseases. Most disease identification requires a compound microscope, preferably with 100x, 200x, and 400x magnification.

Most states provide professional diagnostic services for insect, weed, and disease problems. Some of these services require a modest fee. It may be a very valuable investment in the future of your IPM program to obtain a professional diagnosis of a problem, so that the correct management practices may be chosen.

Instill in the scout the importance of thorough observation, and provide positive reinforcement. For example, whenever the scout notices something that ultimately requires a decision as to whether a control measure will be necessary, include the scout in the decision-making process. Do not underestimate the importance of regular and consistent monitoring of the golf course. "Drive-by scouting" often leads to misdiagnosis. Get off the cart or get out of the truck, and take a closer look.

While most golf course superintendents are already "scouting" their golf courses in some fashion, many fail to maintain consistent and accurate records of those observations. As a result, those observations become anecdotal at best and provide very little guidance in subsequent years. *When in doubt, write it down.*

Even though your written records from previous years are invaluable, they may also be misleading. Problems may have similar symptoms, but require different management approaches. Past records are good clues to this year's problems, but every year is different. Therefore, scouting and monitoring are annual activities to determine the current year's problems and solutions.

MONITORING TECHNIQUES — INSECTS

There are several techniques that can be used to estimate the number of insects present:

Soil Sample (used for billbug larvae, ground pearls, and white grubs) (Figures 3.6 and 3.7)

1. Use a cup-cutter and pull a plug (4.25 inch [11 cm] diameter) or use a shovel to cut three sides of a square, 6 inches (15 cm) on a side.
2. Cut to a depth of about 4 inches (10 cm), and turn the sample over so the soil side is facing up.
3. Break the soil apart gently over a plywood sheet or a cookie sheet, and remove and count any insects in the soil or lower thatch. White grubs will vary in size, depending on the species and the stage of development, but most are between 0.125 and 1 inch (0.3 cm and 2.54 cm) long and can be seen easily against the dark soil. If the soil moisture is adequate for turf growth and soil temperatures are not extreme, most grubs will be within an inch or two of the soil-thatch interface during the growing season.
4. Convert the insect count to "number of insects per square foot" (or other measure) for easy comparison.

Figure 3.6. Monitoring for grubs using a cup cutter to take a soil sample. (Courtesy P.J. Vittum.)

Figure 3.7. Grubs from the sample can be collected on a pie pan for counting. (Courtesy P.J. Vittum.)

- A cup-cutter is 0.1 square foot (so multiply by 10).
- A square, 6 inches on a side, is 0.25 square foot (so multiply by 4).

Soap Flush or Irritating Drench (used for armyworms, cutworms, early stages of green June beetles, earthworms, mole crickets, adult black turfgrass ataenius, and adult annual bluegrass weevils) (Figures 3.8 and 3.9)

1. Add 1 or 2 tablespoons (15–30 mL) of a lemon-scented dish detergent to 1 or 2 gallons (4–8 L) of water. Avoid excessive foam or sudsing.
2. Pour the soapy mix over an area approximately 2 feet (61 cm) on a side.

Insects will be irritated by the soapy solution and wriggle to the surface, usually within five minutes, where they can be counted. Apparently, some of the smallest stages die before they reach the surface. Note that the mixture may burn the turf on hot sunny days if the soapy solution is not rinsed off the surface after the sampling is completed.

Flotation or Flooding (used for chinch bugs)

1. Insert a small cylinder (such as a coffee can) into the turf, to a depth of about 3 or 4 inches (8–10 cm)
2. Fill it with water.

   – or –

Figure 3.8. Application of an irritating drench of soapy water. (Courtesy P.J. Vittum.)

Figure 3.9. Mole crickets on the surface after flushing soil with a soapy solution. (Courtesy P.P. Cobb.)

1. Use a cup-cutter to pull a plug from the area to be sampled.
2. Place the plug in a bucket and fill the bucket with water.

With either method,

3. Insects caught in the flooded area will float to the surface, within the cylinder (or bucket), where they can be counted.

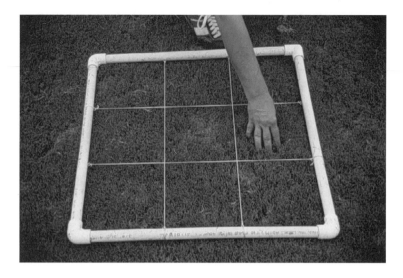

Figure 3.10. Mole cricket rating grid. (Courtesy P.J. Vittum.)

Rating System (used for mole crickets, cutworms) (Figure 3.10)

1. Build a small frame with 0.5–1.0 inch (1.27–2.54 cm) diameter PVC pipe (often 2 feet [61 cm] on a side).
2. Subdivide the frame into 9 equal squares by stringing line from one side of the frame to the opposite side, 2 lines in each direction.
3. Toss the frame on the area to be monitored and conduct the inspection.
4. Inspect each small square visually and manually for evidence of insect burrowing activity. If at least one burrow is found in a given (small) square, that square is given a score of one. For each square that has no activity, a score of zero is assigned. Thus, the total possible score for each placement of the frame will range between zero (no squares showing activity) and nine (activity in all squares).

Repeat the process several times in the vicinity to get an average of insect activity. A rating system will not provide an actual insect count or reveal the stage of development, but it will provide an excellent comparison of insect activity and damage among various areas and from season to season.

Traps

The date of first flight and peak flight, determined by using pheromone or light traps, can be useful as an aid in scheduling control actions.

Pheromone Traps (used for Japanese beetle, black cutworm) (Figure 3.11)

Some female insects produce pheromones (chemicals) which attract males of the same species. Males are attracted to the trap, where they can be counted.

Figure 3.11. Pheromone trap for Japanese beetles. (Courtesy P.J. Vittum.)

Figure 3.12. Light trap for insect monitoring. (Courtesy P.J. Vittum.)

Light Traps (used for moth stages of cutworms, webworms, armyworms, beetle stage of black turfgrass ataenius) (Figure 3.12)

Black (ultraviolet) lights are used to attract night-flying insects, especially moths. Traps are crucial in indicating when moth flights begin in a given area. Since moths sometimes fly in from considerable distances, this information can prove to be invaluable in determining when a pest has arrived for the season (e.g., black cutworms come into the northeastern United States from the southeastern United States each spring). In addition, peak flights in the summer can help a golf course superintendent predict when eggs will be laid and when small caterpillars will be hatching out (and when control measures will be most effective).

Pitfall Traps (used for mobile insects, especially predatory beetles and spiders)

1. Remove a core from the soil and insert a cup or jar of identical diameter in the hole, such that the top of the jar is just below the soil surface.
2. Use a small funnel to pour a non-toxic antifreeze in the jar to a depth of about 1 inch (2.5 cm). (Be careful not to spill the material; it can burn turfgrass.)
3. Remove the jar (one to seven days after it was put in place) and inspect the contents.

Note: This technique is an excellent way to demonstrate the diversity of life in golf course turf to the golfers. Be careful not to use large jars in an area where golfers or others might walk, because they could step in the hole and injure an ankle.

Monitoring Techniques — Diseases

Scout *early* in the morning, when dew is still present, and in the afternoon (Figure 3.13). Observing turf when dew is still present will allow a scout to more easily observe actual fungal mycelia on the leaf tissue. Scouting in the *early afternoon* for localized patches of wilt or drought symptoms may indicate root or crown rot diseases, especially when looking "into the sun."

Important Indications of Disease Problems

Active fungal mycelia (Figures 3.13, 3.14, and 3.15)

- **Color** of mycelia: pink, white, gray
- **Location** of mycelia: small circles, at edge of large patch, or irregular pattern
- **Sclerotia**, spores, or other fungal structures such as those associated with gray snow mold, southern blight, red thread, rust, or smut

Disease symptom patterns

- **Circular patterns** are likely to indicate a fungal disease because many fungi start at a central point and grow out radially (Figure 3.16). This is why most turf disease names include the words "spot" or "patch."
  - Note **size** of circle *and* **location** (near landscaping, pond, high elevations, traffic/compaction areas, etc.)
  - Examine **leaf blades** for lesions.

Figure 3.13. Brown patch with active mycelia in early morning hours when dew is still present. See Color Plate 3. (Courtesy G.L. Schumann.)

Figure 3.14. Characteristic mycelia and spores of the fungus that causes red thread makes diagnosis quite easy in humid weather. See Color Plate 5. (Courtesy G.L. Schumann.)

  – If no lesions are visible on the leaf blades, but the plant is not growing well, examine **roots** and **crowns** for discoloration and decay.
- **Irregular disease patterns** can also occur.
  – Examine individual **leaf blades** for lesions.
  – If no lesions are visible on the leaf blades, but the plant is not growing well, examine **roots** and **crowns** for discoloration and decay.

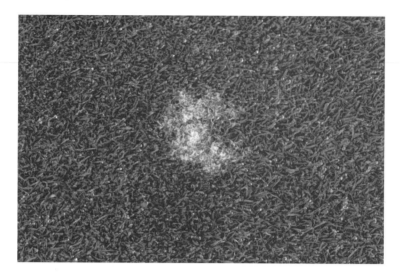

Figure 3.15. In humid weather, the heavy white mycelium of the fungus that causes dollar spot may be easily mistaken for *Pythium*. See Color Plate 6. (Courtesy G.L. Schumann.)

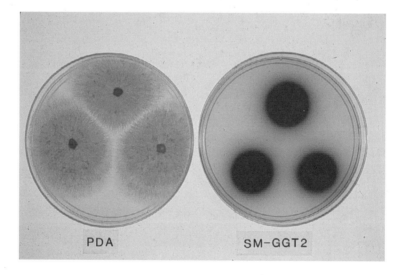

PDA   SM-GGT2

Figure 3.16. In laboratory cultures, fungi grow out radially to form circles. Similarly, many turfgrass disease symptoms commonly occur in a circular pattern of patches or spots. (Courtesy M.L. Elliott.)

Disease Diagnosis

Until a scout becomes *very* familiar with disease symptoms and pathogen identification with a microscope, it is beneficial to have a public or private plant disease diagnostic clinic confirm a suspected disease problem. Many pathogens cause similar plant symptoms. However, management methods are often quite different.

Map Active Disease Sites

Many disease outbreaks occur in the same location each year. Try to correlate disease outbreaks with management operations (e.g., mowing patterns), microenvironments created by landscape around disease-prone areas, or application of pesticides and fertilizers.

When a disease is active, examine the site that is affected by disease on a daily basis. This information, together with weather information, may indicate the potential for disease spread and influence management decisions.

MONITORING TECHNIQUES — NEMATODES

Nematodes are small round worms. Some nematodes are parasites of turfgrass.

Symptoms of nematode injury on turfgrass include:

- Poor growth: sometimes in streaks or circular areas, but often with no pattern
- Susceptibility to wilting
- Root symptoms: lesions, excessive branching, stubby roots, root rot
- Failure to respond to fertilizers or fungicides

Nematode Diagnosis

Nematodes are too small to be seen in soil. Therefore, diagnosis of nematode problems requires laboratory analysis of root and soil samples (Figure 3.17). *All* soil samples contain parasitic nematodes. The *relative numbers* and *kinds* of nematodes determine their role in turf injury.

1. Sample from a number of areas (15–30 soil probe cores to a depth of 4 inches [10 cm]) and then mix the soil together for a composite sample.
2. Place soil samples in a plastic bag, seal, and keep cool and moist until they can be delivered to the laboratory by overnight delivery.
3. Obtain samples from an area showing symptoms of a problem and another set of samples from a nearby area in which the turfgrass is growing well. This pair of samples will help determine if nematodes are the primary problem. If nematode analysis shows similar numbers and kinds in both areas, then nematodes are not likely to be the problem.

Figure 3.17. Soil probe used to sample soil and thatch for nematode assays. (Courtesy P.P. Cobb.)

MONITORING TECHNIQUES — WEEDS

Weed management is based on identification of the weed and a basic understanding of plant biology. A scout must be able to distinguish:

- Grassy vs. broadleaf weeds
- Annual vs. perennial weeds
- Grass-like species (sedges, rushes, wild garlic) vs. true grasses (Figures 3.18 and 3.19)

Three simple techniques can be used to measure or count weeds:

Transect Lines (See Figures 3.20 and 3.21)

1. Lay a rope directly along the area to be sampled or visually identify a point on the opposite side of the area.
2. Walk along the rope (or in the line you have identified), stopping every eight or ten steps.
3. Look at the tip of your foot and determine whether there are any weeds in an imaginary circle of 3 or 4 inch (8 or 10 cm) diameter (about the size of a baseball).
4. Record the number and species on your report sheet (Table 3.2). If you cannot identify them to species, count the number of broadleaf weeds and then the grassy weeds.
5. Calculate the percentage of times when weeds were present out of your total observations (probably between 10 and 20 stopping points).
6. Repeat for as many transect lines as your time permits. More transect lines will provide more information.

Figure 3.18. Sedge weed in turfgrass. (Courtesy M.L. Elliott.)

Figure 3.19. Crabgrass in turfgrass. (Courtesy M.L. Elliott.)

Random Samples

Construct a small ring or frame (perhaps 6 to 8 inches [15–20 cm] on a side or in diameter) with an open center.

1. Toss the sampler onto the turf and inspect all of the turf inside the sampler.
2. Identify weed types as accurately as possible and estimate total coverage within the sample area (e.g., 30% weed-covered).
3. Take several samples from each location.

Both of these techniques will provide numbers of weeds present and indicate weed species present. Compare the results in different areas of the golf

Figure 3.20. Transect line for weed monitoring. (Courtesy J. Bresnahan.)

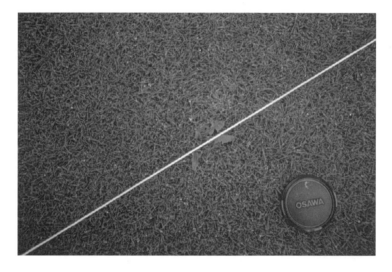

Figure 3.21. Count the weeds that occur along the transect line. (Courtesy J. Bresnahan.)

course or from one season to another or from one year to the next. This information can be used to compare severity of infestation, predict weed activity, or determine if weed management strategies are effective.

Weed Inventory

A walk-through scouting where an inventory of the species is constructed, followed by highlighting the 5 to 8 most important species, can be effective and time-efficient.

FURTHER READING

Baxendale, F.P. and R.E. Gaussoin, Eds. *Integrated Turfgrass Management for the Northern Great Plains.* Cooperative Extension, Institute of Agriculture and Natural Resources, University of Nebraska, Lincoln, NE, 1977.

Brandenburg, R.L. and M.G. Villani. *Handbook of Turfgrass Insects Pests.* Entomological Society of America, Lanham, MD, 1996.

Burpee, L.L. *A Guide to Integrated Control of Turfgrass Diseases, Vol. 1: Cool Season Turfgrasses; Vol. 2: Warm Season Turfgrasses.* GCSAA Press, 1993, 1995.

Couch, H.B. *Diseases of Turfgrasses.* Krieger Publishing, Melbourne, FL, 1995.

Fermanian, T.W., M.C. Shurtleff, R. Randell, H.T. Wilkinson, and P.L. Nixon. *Controlling Turfgrass Pests.* Prentice-Hall, Inc., Upper Saddle River, NJ, 1997.

Hellman, L. The ETs and ATs of Pest-Based Spraying. *Grounds Maintenance.* 27(3):74,76,78,80, 1992.

Leslie, A.R. *Handbook for Integrated Pest Management of Turf and Ornamentals.* Lewis Publishers, Boca Raton, FL, 1994.

Schumann, G.L. and J.D. MacDonald. *Turfgrass Diseases: Diagnosis and Management CD-ROM.* American Phytopathological Society, St. Paul, MN, 1997.

Smiley, R.W., P.H. Dernoeden, and B.B. Clarke. *Compendium of Turfgrass Diseases.* American Phytopathological Society, St. Paul, MN, 1992.

Tani, T. and J.B Beard. *Color Atlas of Turfgrass Diseases.* Ann Arbor Press, Chelsea, MI, 1997.

Tashiro, H. *Turfgrass Insects of the United States and Canada.* Cornell University Press, Ithaca, NY, 1987.

Turgeon, A.J. Ed. *Turf Weeds and Their Control.* American Society of Agronomy and Crop Science Society of America, Madison, WI, 1994.

Vargas, J. *Management of Turfgrass Diseases.* Lewis Publishers, Boca Raton, FL, 1994.

Watschke, T.L., P.H. Dernoeden, and D.J. Shetlar. *Managing Turfgrass Pests.* Lewis Publishers, Boca Raton, FL, 1995.

CHAPTER 4

CULTURAL CONTROL STRATEGIES: STRESS MANAGEMENT

Cultural control strategies have two main goals:

- Alter the microenvironment so it is less favorable for pest and pathogen development or results in suppression of pests and pathogens already present.
- Improve growing conditions of the turfgrass to make it less susceptible to attack by pests and pathogens and to weed invasion.

This means reducing stress!

The following factors affect the turfgrass growing environment and can contribute to plant stress. Stressed plants are more susceptible to injury and infection and will not recover as quickly when damage does occur. Stressed or damaged turf will not be able to outcompete weeds.

MOWING OPERATIONS

Photosynthesis occurs in the leaves and is the sole source of energy (carbohydrates) for plant growth. Mowing removes a portion of the newly emerged leaf blade, leaving older leaves and leaf sheaths behind. Because photosynthetic activity declines with leaf maturity, mowing tends to deprive the plant of its most active leaf tissue.

Mowing allows you to maintain a well-groomed golf course, but it is also a destructive maintenance practice. The reason you can mow turf every day is that the growing points (meristems) are below the mower blade, or should be below the mower blade. If growing points are cut along with leaf blades and sheaths, you have scalped the turf, which ultimately thins the turf.

- Mowing *below* the recommended height (Figures 4.1 and 4.2) means:
  - Slower shoot growth rate.
  - Reduced root growth.
  - Reduced production of defense compounds against pathogens and pests.
  - Reduced recovery after pest injury or disease.
  - Increased encroachment by weeds as the turf weakens.

Figure 4.1. Low mowing height enhances bermudagrass decline in summer: left 3/16" (4.8 mm); right 1/4" (6.4 mm). (Courtesy M.L. Elliott.)

Figure 4.2. Close-up. See Color Plate 7. (Courtesy M.L. Elliott.)

- Mowing *creates* wounds for entry by leaf pathogens.
- Mowing *spreads* leaf pathogens, especially when turfgrass is wet.
- Mowing with clipping removal *increases* fertilizer requirements.
- Mowing frequency and pattern can *increase* stress and compaction.

> *Example:* The "cleanup" pass on a green is often more stressed because the mower goes in the same circle every day.

The Aurora, Colorado municipal golf system includes four 18-hole courses and one par-3 9-hole course. Play is approximately 250,000 rounds annually. Our approach to pest management is to determine threshold tolerance. Our preference is to apply pesticides as infrequently as possible. Before a plant protectant chemical is applied we always ask ourselves the following questions:

1. Can the plant recover on its own without the use of pesticide?

2. While the plant is under attack, does it provide an acceptable playing surface for our customers? (Brown is not necessarily beautiful, but something less than perfect is acceptable.)

3. What alternatives are available other than the use of pesticides to help the plant tolerate the pest? We look primarily at cultural alternatives, i.e., cutting height, cutting frequency, fertilizer application, water usage, etc.

In summary, we have developed an attitude of threshold tolerance toward plant pests. Chemicals are used only after determining that the damage to the plant will exceed threshold tolerance levels.

— Dennis Lyon, CGCS, Aurora, Colorado

WATER MANAGEMENT

Irrigation is essential to prevent drought damage, but the amount of water and the timing of its application are important in reducing disease potential or pest damage, preventing water stress, and ensuring the success of products applied for pest management.

Excessive **irrigation:**

- Increases potential for root diseases and black layer, especially in poorly drained soils.
- Creates high humidity in the canopy, which is conducive to many leaf diseases.
- Leaches nutrients from the soil.
- Provides the water required for weed seeds to germinate and fungal spores to germinate. High humidity encourages fungal sporulation.

Additional problems that result from *excess* water:

- Flooding (Figure 4.3) results in oxygen deficiency in soil, which can reduce root growth and, if prolonged, lead to root death.
- Surface drainage can disperse pathogens and pests across the turfgrass (Figure 4.4).

Figure 4.3. Flooding at a golf course. (Courtesy P.J. Vittum.)

Figure 4.4. Pythium blight spread by water. See Color Plate 8. (Courtesy M.L. Elliott.)

- Sudden freezing of saturated soil and hydrated turfgrass in cold weather can kill turfgrass.
- Pesticides and biological products may become ineffective against soil pests.

Water *deficiency:*

- Weakens turfgrass and makes it more susceptible to injury and disease.
- Reduces photosynthesis, and therefore reduces growth, which slows recovery after injury or disease.

Figure 4.5. Irrigation. (Courtesy P.J. Vittum.)

- Allows winter desiccation to occur in turfgrass exposed to dry winter winds when the soil is frozen. Water lost from the leaf blades cannot be replaced.
- Allows soil insects to move deeper into the soil profile.
- Slows the activity of pesticides and leads to dehydration of biological agents.

Irrigation provides stress relief: (Figure 4.5)

- Brief irrigation (syringing) at mid-day during extended heat stress will cool the plants. It relieves stress without providing sufficient moisture to encourage fungal activity.
- There is some evidence that keeping upper soil layers moist enhances the natural biological control provided by microbial activity against root pathogens.
- Localized dry spots, which may have a biological origin caused by the coating of sand or soil particles with fungal mycelia, may require extensive hand watering and wetting agents in addition to the normal irrigation cycle.

Dew is formed when water from the atmosphere condenses as the leaves become cooler than the air. The dew point is the temperature at which dew will form and is dependent on the relative humidity in the air. It most often forms in the early evening hours when the air cools in the northeastern United States, and usually remains until it evaporates as the morning sun warms the air. Evaporation of dew from turfgrass is slower when the air is very humid, the turf is located in shade, or air circulation is poor.

Guttation fluid may also be part of the dew droplet. Guttation fluid is produced when water pressure from the roots forces plant water to exude through tiny leaf openings called hydathodes and through mowing wounds. This normally occurs during the night. This fluid contains important nutrients which favor the growth of fungi. Most fungi grow poorly or not at all on dry leaf blades.

To keep leaf blades dry as much as possible:

- Whip, pole, or mow dew off early in the morning. (Figure 4.6)
- Irrigate turf in the pre-dawn hours to remove guttation fluid and to avoid lengthening the dew period. (Figure 4.7)
- Avoid irrigation at any time that lengthens the dew period.
- Avoid night watering in hot weather, which favors certain diseases (e.g., Pythium blight, brown patch), especially on disease-prone areas.

Figure 4.6. Chains to drag dew off fairways. (Courtesy P.J. Vittum.)

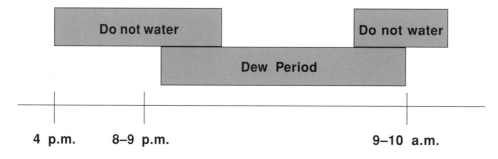

Figure 4.7. Irrigation should be timed to *minimize* the length of time that leaves are wet. This reduces fungal activity and, therefore, foliar diseases. This diagram applies to dew periods typical of the northeastern United States.

- Use fans to increase air circulation.
- Prune or thin landscape plants, especially trees, to increase air circulation.

Irrigation water quality is dependent on its source. For example, effluent water has different types and levels of salts than most well sources or lake sources.

The irrigation water can distinctly affect soil conditions. For example, pH of irrigation water can affect soil pH in upper soil layers where roots are concentrated. It can also affect certain root rot diseases such as take-all patch and summer patch. In addition, there is some evidence that high pH irrigation water may degrade pH-sensitive pesticides.

Therefore, irrigation water should be monitored as closely as one does the soil. Even municipal water sources should be monitored. This way you will know what the "normal" values are for your water source when problems do occur.

Turfgrass IPM in the Arid Southwest:

The PACE Turfgrass Research Institute conducts research to discover and develop management practices that reduce plant stress while maintaining a high quality golfing experience.

Traffic: The greatest stress-inducing event that occurs on a golf course is the plant and soil damage caused by the golfer foot traffic and golf carts. Traffic results in compacted soils, reduced water infiltration, elevated soil CO_2 and reduced O_2, and direct plant damage. In many cases, fungicide applications on greens can be avoided with effective traffic control, which results in reduced compaction and reduced plant stress. To combat compaction and to improve water infiltration and gas exchange, monthly small-diameter (0.25 inch) aeration is encouraged. The small aeration holes heal rapidly and result in only limited interference with golf play.

Irrigation Management and Soil Salinity: Second to compaction in importance for reducing fungicide applications is irrigation and salinity management. In an arid environment, free water is a critical requirement for disease development. If the irrigation is applied properly, diseases can be limited and sometimes eliminated.

However, a typical irrigation program delivers about 600 pounds of salt to a 5,000-ft^2 green per year. This salt level will increase soil salinity to levels that exceed the tolerance of annual bluegrass and bentgrass greens (8 dS/m in the top 3 inches). In order to reduce soil salt levels, leaching irrigation frequently results in more than 12 hours of free moisture on foliage, which is conducive to many diseases, including anthracnose and Pythium blight. During warm summer months, preventive fungicide applications are recommended prior to leaching events.

IPM is a step in the right direction toward more effective and environmentally sound turfgrass management practices. However, IPM will only result in reduced risk pest management when the health of the plant is thoroughly understood and cultural practices are improved to allow the plant to effectively resist diseases, tolerate insects, and compete with weeds.

— Dr. Larry Stowell, PACE-PTRI, San Diego, California

SELECTION OF TURFGRASS SPECIES AND CULTIVARS

Genetic resistance is an important component of any IPM program. Turfgrass species and cultivars of these species possess genetic traits that allow managers to select plants that can be grown successfully in a particular environment. Make use of your *local* recommendations because they will include evaluation of the performance of various cultivars in *your* environment when exposed to *your* predominant pest and disease problems (Figure 4.8).

The following factors are important in making turfgrass selections for initial plantings, renovations, and overseeding.

Environmental adaptation to:

- Cold
- Heat
- Drought
- High humidity and rainfall
- Salinity
- Soil pH
- Shade/sun
- Soil types/drainage

Adaptation to anticipated uses and maintenance practices:

- Use of greens, tees, fairways, and roughs
- Overall aesthetics and budget
- Mowing height
- Fertilizer requirements
- Water requirements
- Thatch tendency
- Wear resistance
- Recuperative capacity
- Cultivation practices

Figure 4.8. Cultivar evaluation trial of bermudagrasses maintained as putting greens mowed at 1/8" (3 mm). See Color Plate 9. (Courtesy M.L. Elliott.)

Insect resistance:

Turfgrass cultivars with endophytes are resistant to some foliar-feeding insects and may have increased disease tolerance to certain diseases, such as dollar spot and summer patch. Endophytes are beneficial fungi that live in the leaves of turfgrass plants. Currently, endophytes are only available in some perennial ryegrass and fescue cultivars, but research is underway to identify or incorporate endophytes into other turfgrass species (Figure 4.9). See Chapter 5 for further information.

Disease resistance or tolerance: (Figure 4.10)

- Select turfgrass species and their cultivars based on the most important diseases in *your* area.
- When overseeding or renovating areas where a particular disease is a chronic problem, select turfgrass species or specific cultivars of turfgrass species with genetic resistance to that disease.

  Example: Perennial ryegrass may be a good choice for fairways where summer patch is a severe disease problem because it is not susceptible to that disease.

FERTILIZATION

Fertilizer products (organic and inorganic) should be selected based on nutrient requirements of the turfgrass and not on any *potential* secondary attributes.

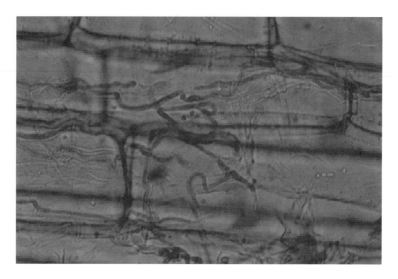

Figure 4.9. Mycelium (threadlike filaments) of a fungal endophyte in a turfgrass leaf blade. (Courtesy R.L. Wick.)

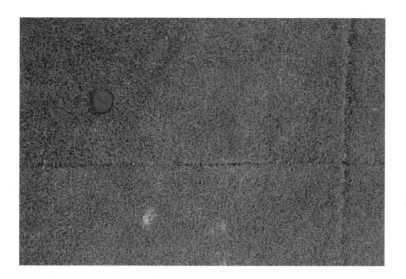

Figure 4.10. Brown patch (*Rhizoctonia solani*) resistance in creeping bentgrass (healthy plots) compared to colonial bentgrass plot (diseased plot). See Color Plate 10. (Courtesy G.L. Schumann.)

Fertility deficiencies, excesses, and imbalances:

- Reduce growth
- Reduce stress tolerance
- Increase potential for injury from insect pests
- Increase susceptibility to certain diseases
- Increase incidence of certain weed species
- Slow recovery from injury, wear, and disease

Figure 4.11. These naturally infected plots vary only in the amount of nitrogen fertilizer they have received. The low-nitrogen plot on the right has dollar spot; the high-nitrogen plot on the left has brown patch. See Color Plate 11. (Courtesy G.L. Schumann.)

Examples

- Fall armyworms are attracted to lush (overfertilized, especially with nitrogen) grass.
- Weakened turf is open to weed infestations. Legume weeds (e.g., clover) are common in low-nitrogen areas because they can provide their own nitrogen.
- Some diseases are more common in low-nitrogen turf (dollar spot, red thread); other diseases are enhanced in overfertilized turf (brown patch, leaf spot) (Figure 4.11).

While nitrogen receives most of the attention, potassium levels should not be overlooked. Potassium has been recognized for its ability to improve plant resistance to disease, drought, cold temperatures, and traffic.

Potassium plays a very important role in many physiological functions, including:

- Photosynthesis
- Respiration
- Protein and carbohydrate metabolism
- Water regulation
- Enzyme activity

Micronutrients are important for turfgrass health and vigor. There are great regional differences in plant nutritional requirements that are influenced by soil types and season. Consult local specialists for more detailed information.

Figure 4.12. Core aeration. (Courtesy F.D. Dinelli.)

Soil pH is an important factor in fertility because it affects the *availability* of nutrients, especially micronutrients, to the turfgrass. At pH extremes, some nutrients become much less available, while others become available at toxic levels.

Note: Fertilization practices and timing vary greatly from one climatic region to another, and depend on the turfgrass species grown. Develop a program that fits *your* management goals.

ABIOTIC SOIL FACTORS

In many cases, fairways are native soil, but the greens and tees are built with a root-zone mix of sand and organic matter that is not a true soil and does not develop traditional soil characteristics for many years. Aeration (Figure 4.12) and drainage are critical for optimal turfgrass health. Soil must hold sufficient water and also contain air pores to provide oxygen for root growth.

Many turf problems begin in the root zone and can be traced to soil conditions. A soil probe should be the IPM scout's best friend!

Important soil factors (chemical and physical) include:

- **Soil pH** — a measure of the acidity or alkalinity of the soil on a scale from 0 to 14. A value of 7 is defined as neutral; values below 7 are acid; values above 7 are basic (or alkaline). Most turfgrasses are best adapted to a pH range from 5.5 to 7.8.
- **Soil type** — defined by the relative amounts of sand, silt, and clay particles in a soil. Sandy soils have larger particles and larger soil pores, which results in faster drainage and poor nutrient retention.
- **Compaction** — results from traffic, which packs soil particles together and reduces the soil pore space so drainage is impeded and oxygen supply to roots is reduced.

Figure 4.13. Close-up of removed soil cores. (Courtesy F.D. Dinelli.)

Figure 4.14. Breaking up core plugs. (Courtesy F.D. Dinelli.)

- **Salinity** — is a measure of salt content in the soil and is a particular concern in drier regions where irrigation water or rainfall is restricted.
- **Thatch** — the layer of organic materials that accumulates between the green, living vegetation of turf and the soil surface (Figures 4.15 and 4.16).
- **Cation exchange capacity** — the total amount of exchangeable cations that the soil can absorb; a measure of CEC reflects the ability of the soil to retain nutrients.
- **Nutrient levels** — can be determined by laboratories from soil tests and leaf tissue tests to help guide fertilizer needs.

Figure 4.15. Thatch layer in turf that has not been cultivated in more than one year. See Color Plate 12. (Courtesy M.L. Elliott.)

Figure 4.16. Optimal uniform organic layer in soil when aeration is performed regularly. See Color Plate 13. (Courtesy M.L. Elliott.)

Obtain soil samples on a regular basis to provide a history of that soil. Whenever possible, soil samples should be sent to the same laboratory in order to obtain comparable results over time. *Soil samples should be used together with leaf tissue analysis to determine the need for specific nutrients.* If the laboratory you use is not familiar with golf course turfgrass, then do not rely on it for interpretation of your results. Learn how to make your own interpretation of results based on your knowledge of your golf course.

FURTHER READING

Beard, J.B. Turf Regrowth. *Grounds Maintenance.* 27(5):36–38, 1992.

Beard, J.B. Turfgrass Heat Stress: What Can Be Done? *Golf Course Management.* 63(12):52–55, 1995.

Beard, J.B. Turfgrass Management for Golf Course. MacMillan Co., New York, NY, 1982, 642 pages.

Beard, J.B. Turfgrass: Science and Culture. Regents/Prentice Hall. Englewood Cliffs, NJ, 1973, 658 pages.

Carrow, R.N. Wear Stress on Turfgrass. *Golf Course Management.* 3(9):49–53, 1995.

Carrow, R.N. Soil Testing for Fertilizer Recommendations. *Golf Course Management.* 63(11):61–68, 1995.

Christians, N.E. Phosphorus Nutrition of Turfgrass. *Golf Course Management.* 64(2):54–57, 1996.

Cobb, P.P. Insect Control on the Golf Course: A Major Linkage with Irrigation. *Golf Course Irrigation.* 4(2):12–14, 1996.

Danneberger, T.K. *Turfgrass Ecology and Management.* Franzak & Foster, GIE, Cleveland, OH, 1993.

Elliott, M.L. Managing Disease Pressures. *Golf Course Management.* 63(5):49–53, 1995.

Hagan, A. Irrigation and its Impact on Turfgrass Diseases. *Golf Course Irrigation.* 4(5):12–14, 1996.

Hayes, A. Comparing Well Water with Effluent: What Superintendents Need to Know. *Golf Course Management.* 63(6):49–53, 1995.

Hull, R. Nitrate Leaching from Turf. *TurfGrass Trends.* 4(2):1–9, 1995.

Lubin, T. Controlling Soil pH with Irrigation Water. *Golf Course Management.* 6(11):56–60, 1995.

Nus, J. Potassium. *Golf Course Management.* 63(1):55–58, 1995.

Richardson, M.D. and C.W. Bacon. Stress Tolerance of Endophyte-Infected Turfgrass, in *Handbook of Integrated Pest Management for Turf and Ornamentals.* Leslie, A.R., Ed., Lewis Publishers, Boca Raton, FL, 1994.

Ruemmele, B. *Poa annua* Management. *TurfGrass Trends.* 5(3):11–15, 1996.

Stowell, L.J. How Does Your Irrigation Water Measure Up? *Golf Course Management.* 63(6):58–62, 1995.

Turgeon, A.J. *Turfgrass Management.* Prentice-Hall, Englewood Cliffs, NJ, 1991.

CHAPTER 5
BIOLOGICAL CONTROL STRATEGIES

Biological control (also called biocontrol) refers to the use of living organisms or by-products of living organisms to suppress pest or pathogen populations. Some of the turf pests, especially *insects* and *weeds,* which occur on golf courses in the United States have naturally occurring enemies (predators or parasites or pathogens) which help suppress the pest population. In many cases, however, the turf pest originated somewhere else in the world. When the pest was imported (usually accidentally) to the United States, its natural enemies did not make the journey at the same time. There may be natural enemies in the United States which can attack the pest. If not, it may be necessary to travel to the place where the pest originated, look for natural enemies in its home setting, test those natural enemies for suitability, and ultimately release them in the "new" location.

> *Example:* The Japanese beetle has become a serious pest east of the Mississippi River. The adults feed on over 300 species of trees and shrubs, and the grubs attack turf roots. The Japanese beetle is not a serious pest in Japan because several parasites and predators attack the beetle and keep its populations below damaging levels. Some of those natural enemies have been released in parts of the United States and have had varying degrees of success at reducing beetle populations.

Biocontrol of turfgrass *diseases* usually involves the use of various microorganisms that can inhibit or outcompete the fungi that cause disease. In some cases, specific microorganisms are applied to the turf in methods similar to a traditional fungicide application; in other cases, organic materials are applied to turf to enhance the populations of beneficial organisms. Biocontrol of *weeds* using pests and pathogens is still in its early stages, but considerable potential exists.

It is unlikely that any biological control approach will give the rapid and dramatic results of most traditional pesticides. However, there is no doubt that some pesticides can cause non-target effects that may be detrimental to the environment and may, in some cases, result in increased risk of subsequent pest and disease outbreaks. Biological control offers the opportunity to reduce the use of traditional chemical pesticides and, perhaps, moderate some of the detrimental non-target effects. Biological control will be most effective when used in conjunction with improved cultural practices and increased tolerance levels for pests and diseases. Some introductory information about biocontrol of insects, diseases, and weeds follows. More detailed information is available in the specific chapters on insects, diseases, and weeds.

> IPM is the *focal point* by which our turf is managed. The balance between chemical, mechanical, and natural tools is utilized to the utmost to maintain the high quality demanded by our golfing community.
>
> Our fertilizer program has changed to the use of coated slow-release formulations, which has allowed for a reduction in quantity applied and yet given better performance. We are constantly in search of biologicals that will fit our aquatic environment, as we tend to steer away from herbicides unless deemed necessary. IPM is our mainstay.
>
> — James W. Dusin, Greenkeeper, Apple Tree Golf Course, Yakima, Washington

INSECT BIOCONTROL

Several kinds of organisms or by-products of living organisms suppress insect populations. Some of these organisms are produced on a large scale and are available commercially, while others are still in development for commercial release. Some of the biocontrol agents can be used in a manner very similar to that of traditional insecticides (i.e., apply through a hydraulic sprayer and expect a reduction of the pest population within a few days) while others may seem quite different (i.e., apply by hand and anticipate a delayed effect). The following categories of biocontrol agents are available or in development for turfgrass insect pests:

Parasites

Parasites are small insects which feed internally on target insects (Figures 5.1 and 5.2).

Characteristics:

- Parasite female lays eggs on or inside target insect.
- Larvae hatch out and feed on internal tissues of target insect.
- Usually flies or wasps.

Advantage:

- Often host-specific (parasitize one or a few pest species, so do not interfere with other beneficial insects).

Figure 5.1. Japanese beetle with eggs laid by a parasitic tachinid fly, called the "winsome fly" (*Hyperecteina aldrichi*). (Courtesy P.J. Vittum.)

Figure 5.2. Third instar June beetle grub (*Phyllophaga* sp.) parasitized by tachinid fly larvae. See Color Plate 14. (Courtesy M.G. Villani.)

Disadvantages:

- Each parasite is involved in the death of only one "victim."
- Parasite and target insect must be at the right stage of development for successful invasion.
- Often sensitive to broad-spectrum insecticides.

Examples:

- Winsome fly (*Hyperecteina aldrichi*) on Japanese beetle adults.
- Parasitic wasps (*Tiphia* spp.) on white grubs.
- Red-eyed Brazilian fly (*Ormia depleta*) on mole crickets.

Predators

Predators are insects that search out and attack target pests (Figure 5.3).

Characteristics:

- Adult and/or immature stages which are mobile.
- May have chewing or sucking mouthparts.
- Usually beetles, true bugs, or spiders (not true insects).

Advantages:

- Each predator accounts for the deaths of many (sometimes more than 1,000) "victims."
- Often "generalists," feeding on a variety of insects (survival is not linked to a single host).

Disadvantages:

- Often sensitive to broad-spectrum insecticides.
- Predator and target insect must be at the right stage of development for successful invasion.

Examples:

- Ladybird (lady bug) beetles on aphids and other soft bodied insects.
- Ground beetles on eggs and small stages of caterpillars.
- Spiders on a variety of insects.

Pathogens

Pathogens are organisms that cause insects to become diseased (Figures 5.4, 5.5, and 5.6).

Entomopathogenic nematodes — tiny worm-like animals which penetrate insect bodies through natural body openings and release bacteria which then cause disease in the target insect (Figure 5.4).

Characteristics:

- Not harmful to plants.
- Small but mobile, so they can sense the presence of an insect and move toward it.

Figure 5.3. Big-eyed bug (*Geocoris* sp.), a generalist insect predator of chinch bugs and other turf insects. (Courtesy M.G. Villani.)

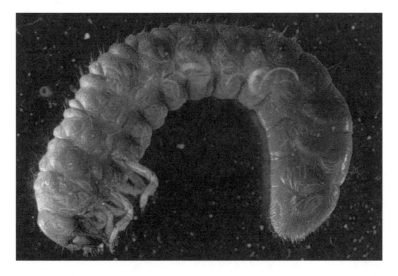

Figure 5.4. Third instar Japanese beetle grub infected by the nematode *Heterorhabditis bacteriophora*. Both infective immatures (dauers) and adult nematodes are visible. See Color Plate 15. (Courtesy M.G. Villani.)

Advantages:

- Can be applied through standard spray equipment (although sometimes fine filters should be replaced by coarser filters).
- Some may kill target pests in less than a week.
- Appear to be effective against various caterpillars and mole crickets.
- Can reproduce throughout the growing season and maintain a population.

Figure 5.5. Third instar black turfgrass ataenius grub with milky disease caused by a *Bacillus* bacterium (right), compared to a healthy grub (left). See Color Plate 16. (Courtesy M.G. Villani.)

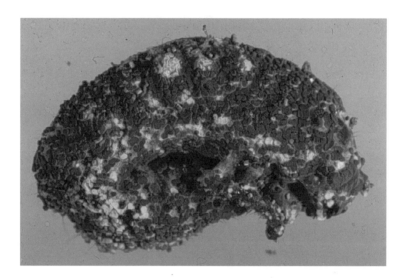

Figure 5.6. Third instar Japanese beetle grub infected by the fungus *Metarhizium anisopliae*. See Color Plate 17. (Courtesy M.G. Villani.)

- Very low level of toxicity to vertebrates.
- Used for suppression of target pests in environmentally sensitive areas.

Disadvantages:

- Very sensitive to desiccation (should not be applied at midday; must be watered in immediately after application).
- Shelf life (3 to 6 months for most formulations) is shorter than most traditional insecticides.

- Must be stored at moderate temperatures.
- Cannot be applied through high-pressure liquid injection systems.
- Repeat applications may be necessary, so total cost may be higher than with traditional insecticides.
- Timing of application even more critical than with traditional insecticides.
- Often not effective against all stages of insects.
- Level of control may be lower than expected with traditional insecticides.

Examples:

- *Steinernema carpocapsae* (BioSafe, Vector, and other trade names) on cutworms, webworms; possibly on billbugs and some weevils.
- *Steinernema glaseri* on white grubs (not yet commercially developed).
- *Steinernema riobravis* (Vector MC) on mole crickets.
- *Steinernema scapterisci* (Proactant) on mole crickets.
- *Heterorhabditis bacteriophora* (Cruiser) on white grubs, billbugs.

Bacteria — microscopic organisms which produce toxins that are specific for the target insect(s). Either live bacteria (BP — see below) are ingested by the target insect, and the toxin is produced in the insect's gut, or the toxin itself (BT — see below) is applied to the turf and the insect ingests the toxin. In either case, the toxins paralyze or otherwise interfere with digestion in the insect (Figure 5.5).

Characteristics:

- Some kill target insects quickly; others work very slowly.
- Some are specific, affecting only a few kinds of insects; others are relatively general.
- Some persist in the soil for several years; others are short-lived.

Advantages:

- Not detrimental to most beneficial insects in turf.
- Very low level of toxicity to vertebrates.

Disadvantages:

- Will take several days (BT) to several months (BP) to kill target insect.
- Timing is critical: applications *must* be made when target insects are in smallest, immature stages.
- Infection rate of milky disease (on Japanese beetle grubs) can be very inconsistent.

Examples:

- *Bacillus thuringiensis* (BT) var. *israelensis* (Bactimos, Technar, Vectobac) on mosquitoes.
- *Bacillus thuringiensis* (BT) var. *kurstaki* (Dipel, Javelin, Steward, and others) on cutworms, webworms.
- *Bacillus thuringiensis* (BT) var. *japonensis* ("*buibui*") on some species of annual white grubs.
- *Bacillus popilliae* (BP) (milky disease, available commercially as Doom, Japidemic) on Japanese beetle grubs.

Fungi — Several kinds of fungi occur naturally in the soil or thatch and attack insects. They are incapable of attacking plants. (Figure 5.6)

Characteristics:

- Some are generalists and attack several different kinds of insects.
- Often favored by moist and relatively cool conditions.
- Some produce distinctive mycelia and spores (e.g., cotton candy appearance) on infected insects.
- Spores produced on infected insects serve to disperse the fungus to its next victims.

Advantages:

- Very low level of toxicity to vertebrates.
- Once established, may persist.

Disadvantages:

- Some formulations are sensitive to breakdown in sunlight.
- Not yet available commercially for use on turf.

Examples:

- *Beauvaria bassiana* on chinch bugs and billbugs.
- *Metarhizium anisopliae* on white grubs.

Problem: The number one insect problem in Florida is the mole cricket. At Doral, I could not control mole crickets because the lights around the resort's buildings attracted the mole crickets. Insecticides alone were only providing about 50% control.

Solution: With the help of Dr. Howard Frank at the University of Florida in Gainesville, we introduced the red-eyed Brazilian fly (*Ormia depleta*) on one of Doral's courses. The fly locates mole crickets by their singing and deposits live maggots on or near the cricket. The maggots then kill the mole cricket. In order for the fly to establish, it needed lots of flowering plants. That was no problem at Doral due to our extensive use of flowering plants in the landscape.

Results: After we introduced the fly, we had 90–95% control of our mole cricket problem on this course. We know it was the integrated use of insecticides and red-eyed flies that controlled the mole crickets, because one of the other courses at Doral that was *not* involved with the red-eyed fly introduction still had an uncontrollable mole cricket problem.

— Steven Kuhn, High Ridge Country Club, Palm Beach County, Florida (formerly with Doral Golf Resort & Spa, Dade County, Florida)

Insect Growth Regulators (IGRs)

Insect growth regulators are products which interfere with an insect's ability to molt from one stage to the next.

"Juvenile hormones" are IGRs which occur naturally in an insect and signal the insect that it is not yet time to molt to the adult stage. Juvenile hormones prevent an insect from reaching the adult stage, so it is unable to reproduce. Other IGRs interfere with the production of chitin or other materials critical to the formation of the insect cuticle.

Characteristics:

- Juvenile hormones tend to be quite specific, affecting only a few closely related insects.
- Chitin inhibitors tend to be less specific.
- Some IGRs work very slowly, preventing successful molts (Figure 5.7), but they do not kill the insect directly.

Advantages:

- Juvenile hormones do not have a detrimental effect on most beneficial insects.
- Most IGRs are virtually non-toxic to vertebrates.

Disadvantages:

- Chitin inhibitors can be broad-spectrum and affect beneficial organisms.
- Some are sensitive to sunlight.
- Commercial formulations have been difficult to produce.

Figure 5.7. Third instar Japanese beetle grub that failed to molt properly when treated with an insect growth regulator (IGR). See Color Plate 18. (Courtesy M.G. Villani.)

- Azadirachitin must be applied when the target insect is in relatively small, immature stages.

Examples:

- Azadirachitin or neem (Turplex, Bioneem, Azatin) on cutworms, webworms.
- Halofenozide (Mach 2) on white grubs.
- Methoprene (Altosid) on mosquito larvae.

Endophytes

Endophytes are fungi which grow inside plants and produce compounds that are toxic to surface-feeding insects such as chinch bugs, cutworms, webworms, and billbugs; also toxic to grazing livestock.

Characteristics:

- Used at time of turfgrass establishment or overseeding by planting endophyte-infected seed.
- Seed must be kept cool and used within 9 months to maintain high levels of the endophytic fungus.
- Seed sources specify the percentage of endophyte seed in each lot.
- Endophyte fungus is seedborne and does not spread to neighboring plants.
- Endophytic grasses planted in areas with high pest insect pressure will tend to spread as non-endophytic grasses are killed.

Advantages:

- Endophytic cultivars often are more heat and drought tolerant than the same cultivar without endophyte.
- Apparently no detrimental effect on beneficial insects.
- Once established, remains viable for the life of the plant.
- Endophytic cultivars may be more tolerant of certain diseases, such as dollar spot and summer patch.

Disadvantages:

- Can be toxic to grazing livestock (effect on dogs and cats still undetermined but presumed to be minimal; is more likely to be a problem for animals whose sole food source is grass).
- Not yet available in bentgrasses, bluegrasses, bermudagrasses.
- Established turfgrass plants cannot be infected with the endophyte fungus.

Examples:

- Some perennial ryegrass cultivars.
- Some fine-leaf fescues and tall fescue cultivars.

(See Chapter 7 for more detailed information.)

DISEASE BIOCONTROL

Natural Biological Control

The microorganisms naturally present in the turfgrass ecosystem help reduce the potential for disease by competing with pathogens and/or by producing chemicals that inhibit the growth of pathogens.

Evidence for this "natural" biological control includes:

1. *The sporadic nature of disease.*
   Diseases do not occur every time environmental conditions are conducive for development.
2. *Disease resurgence after fungicide use.*
   Fungicides kill or inhibit a variety of fungi, not only those that cause turf diseases. As a result, sometimes a disease outbreak is greater in areas where a fungicide was used previously than in areas where no fungicide was used.

3. *The natural decline of some diseases several years after the initial severe outbreaks* (e.g., necrotic ring spot, summer patch, take-all patch).

   This is thought to occur because of the natural increase over time of a microbial population that helps control the pathogens.

4. *In university experiments, necrotic ring spot was controlled by brief mid-day irrigation.*

   This technique is thought to reduce plant heat stress and to maintain soil moisture for increased microbial activity.

5. *The increase of certain diseases when fungicides are applied to control another disease.*

   This suggests that certain fungicide applications can cause a temporary ecological imbalance, so that diseases that are not controlled by the fungicide may actually be enhanced by its use.

Introduced Biological Control

Some commercial biological control products for turfgrass diseases have recently become available, but their successful use in commercial turfgrass management has not been widely demonstrated. Numerous biocontrol strategies that are already available or are in the research stage and show promise of eventual practical use include:

1. Introduction of **specific microorganisms** that will prevent or reduce certain turfgrass diseases by producing toxic compounds or outcompeting the pathogenic fungi.

   Commercial products:

   Biotrek 22G — a granular formulation of an isolate of the fungus *Trichoderma harzianum* (Wilbur-Ellis Co., Fresno California).
   BioJect — a mechanism that delivers large populations of the bacterium *Pseudomonas aureofaceans* through the irrigation system (EcoSoil Systems, Inc., San Diego, California) (Figure 5.8).
   Companion — a liquid formulation of *Bacillus* bacteria that is mixed with water and applied to turf (Growth Products Ltd., White Plains, New York).

   Successful research demonstrations:

   Non-pathogenic strains of fungi closely related to fungi that cause turfgrass diseases:
           Binucleate *Rhizoctonia* spp. for brown patch
           Typhula phacorrhiza for gray snow mold

Figure 5.8. BioJect biocontrol system. (Courtesy F.D. Dinelli.)

Numerous isolates of the bacterium *Enterobacter cloacae*, other bacteria, and fungi.

2. Application of organic materials (e.g., composts) that contain **populations of microorganisms** which may reduce turfgrass disease development (Figures 5.9 and 5.10).

(See Chapter 8 for more detailed information on biological controls for turfgrass diseases.)

WEED BIOCONTROL

No commercial products are currently available for the biological control of weeds. Possible agents include insect pests and pathogens, such as bacteria and fungi. A bacterium, *Xanthomonas campestris*, has been tested as a biocontrol for annual bluegrass (Figure 5.11). It has had some success in the desert Southwest but not in the northeastern United States. Some species of the fungal genus *Sclerotinia* have been tested for their ability to attack broadleaf turfgrass weeds such as dandelion. Potential weed biocontrol agents must attack the weed similarly to a chemical herbicide in order to sufficiently weaken these aggressive turfgrass competitors.

Figure 5.9. Topdressing fairways with compost. (Courtesy F.D. Dinelli.)

Figure 5.10. Compost coverage at a rate of 10 cubic yards per acre. (Courtesy F.D. Dinelli.)

Corn gluten is marketed as a natural organic fertilizer with some non-selective, pre-emergent herbicidal activity. A number of studies have been conducted to determine its ability to control crabgrass, with mixed results.

A major limitation to weed biocontrols is that many parasites are quite specific in their host range. This is an advantage as a biocontrol because the agent will infect the weed but not the turfgrass. However, this same specificity means that several different biocontrol agents will probably be necessary for the various weed species that require management.

The intensive management of turfgrass and the ability to modify the environment to enhance the activity of the biocontrol agent favors the future success of weed biocontrol in turfgrasses. Biocontrol of weeds is not likely to offer

Figure 5.11. Recovery of *Poa annua* spp. *reptans* following inoculation with the bacterium *Xanthomonas campestris* pv. *poannua* in a biocontrol experiment. (Courtesy J.C. Neal.)

the same level of control as herbicides, but it may be acceptable where weed tolerance is greater and/or where chemical control is not tolerated.

FURTHER READING

Burpee, L.L. A Method of Assessing the Efficacy of a Biocontrol Agent on Dandelion (*Taraxacum officinale*). *Weed Technol.* 6:401–403, 1992.

Christians, N.E. A Natural Product for the Control of Annual Weeds. *Golf Course Management.* 61(10):72–76, 1993.

Fraser, M.L. and J.P. Breen. The Role of Endophytes in IPM for Turf, in *Handbook of Integrated Pest Management for Turf and Ornamentals*, Leslie, A.R., Ed., Lewis Publishers, Boca Raton, FL, 1994.

Georgis, R. and G.O. Poinar, Jr. Nematodes as Bioinsecticides in Turf and Ornamentals, in *Handbook of Integrated Pest Management for Turf and Ornamentals*, Leslie, A.R., Ed., Lewis Publishers, Boca Raton, FL, 1994.

Johnson, B.J. 1994. Biological Control of Annual Bluegrass with *Xanthomonas campestris* pv. *poannua*. *HortScience.* 29:659–662, 1992.

Klein, M.G. Microbial Control of Turfgrass Insects, in *Handbook of Turfgrass Insect Pests*, Brandenburg, R.L. and M.G. Villani, Eds., Entomological Society of America, Lanham, MD, 1995.

Nelson, E.B. Enhancing Turfgrass Disease Control with Organic Amendments. *TurfGrass Trends.* 5(6):1–15, 1996.

Nelson, E.B., L.L. Burpee, and M.B. Lawton. Biological Control of Turfgrass Diseases, in *Handbook of Integrated Pest Management for Turf and Ornamentals*, Leslie, A.R., Ed., Lewis Publishers, Boca Raton, FL, 1994.

Phatak, S.C., D.R. Sumner, H.D. Wells, D.K. Bell, and N.C. Glaze. Biological Control of Yellow Nutsedge with the Indigenous Rust Fungus *Puccinia canaliculata*. *Science* 219:1446–1447, 1983.

Riddle, G.E., L.L. Burpee, and G.J. Boland. Virulence of *Sclerotinia sclerotiorum* and *S. minor* on dandelion (*Taraxacum officinale*). *Weed Sci.* 39:109–118, 1991.

Shetlar, D.J. Field Testing of Biological Pesticides. *TurfGrass Trends.* 5(8):1–9, 1996.

Sun, S. Endophytes for Creeping Bentgrass and Kentucky Bluegrass. *Golf Course Management.* 64(9):49–52, 1996.

Villani, M.G. Focus on Biological Controls (Insects). *TurfGrass Trends.* 4(6):1–6, 1995.

Weinzierl, R. and T. Henn. Beneficial Insects and Mites, in *Handbook of Integrated Pest Management for Turf and Ornamentals*, Leslie, A.R., Ed., Lewis Publishers, Boca Raton, FL, 1994.

Zhou, T. and J.C. Neal. Annual Bluegrass (*Poa annua*) Control with *Xanthomonas campestris* pv. *poannua* in New York State. *Weed Technology.* 9:173–177, 1995.

CHAPTER 6

CHEMICAL CONTROL STRATEGIES

Pesticides play an important role in an Integrated Pest Management program when cultural practices and biological control efforts are insufficient to maintain pest populations at an acceptable level or other factors conspire to raise pest populations above threshold levels. For example, very disease-conducive weather conditions may overwhelm even the best cultural programs for disease management. Pesticide decisions are complicated and include consideration of these factors:

- Environmental risks
- Timing of application for optimal effect
- Characteristics of the pesticide
- Water quality and amounts required
- Spectrum of activity
- Resistance management
- Sensitivity to microbial degradation
- State and local regulations

Most pesticide failures are due to misapplication of the product or use of the wrong product. Read the entire label. Remember: The label is the law. It is critical to also know the *local* recommendations for each product. Before you randomly mix pesticides (and/or fertilizers) together, review the chemistry of adjuvants and tank mixes.

> IPM isn't a cure-all or end-all for pesticide use. Sometimes the expectation of perfection forces one to rely on the use of pesticides.
>
> — Donald E. Hearn, CGCS, Weston Golf Club, Weston, Massachusetts

ENVIRONMENTAL RISKS

The following potential risks should be considered in pesticide decisions:

Runoff

Runoff is the lateral movement of a pesticide in water.

Figure 6.1. Aerification of a pond at Country Club of Lincoln (Nebraska). (Courtesy P.J. Vittum.)

Factors that *increase* the risk of runoff:

- Water solubility of the pesticide
  More soluble compounds are more likely to run off.
- Proximity to surface water (e.g., stream, pond)
- Soil compaction
  Compacted soils cannot absorb as much water and so are more likely to experience runoff.
- Steep slope
  Water, and therefore pesticides in water, will move more readily on steep slopes.
- Intense rain or irrigation

To *minimize* risk of runoff:

- Use less soluble pesticides, if available.
- Leave untreated buffer zones near surface waters.
- Do not treat steeply sloped and/or compacted areas.
- Avoid overirrigation. Break irrigation into two or more periods.
- Do not apply pesticides during or before an expected intense rain.

Leaching

Leaching is the vertical movement of a pesticide in water through the soil profile.

Factors that *increase* risk of leaching:

- Water solubility of the pesticide
  More soluble pesticides are more likely to leach.
- Persistence of the pesticide
  Longer lasting compounds are more likely to reach groundwater sources.
- Sandy soils
  Pesticides in water move more readily through sandy soils than clayey soils.
- Shallow water table
  If the water table is shallow, rain or irrigation water does not have to travel very far to reach the water table.
- Rainy climate
- Little vegetative cover in the area treated
  Roots and other organic matter act like sponges, absorbing water and slowing its movement.

To *minimize* risk of leaching:

- Use less soluble pesticides, if available.
- Use less persistent pesticides.
- Maintain dense turfgrass.
- Avoid applications to bare soil.
- Avoid overirrigation.
- Do not apply pesticides during or before an expected intense rain, especially on sandy soils.

Volatilization

Volatilization is the "evaporation" of a pesticide from soil or turf into the atmosphere.

Factors that *increase* risk of volatilization:

- Volatility of pesticide (determined by chemical properties and formulation)
- Air movement
- Low relative humidity
- Warm temperatures

To *minimize* risk of volatilization:

- Use granular formulations of pesticide.
- Apply appropriate irrigation after an application.

Figure 6.2. Collecting clippings, Sleepy Hollow Country Club, Scarborough, New York. (Courtesy P.J. Vittum.)

- Avoid applications in hot, dry, or windy conditions.
- Treat in late afternoon or evening.

Accumulation in Clippings

Although most pesticides available today degrade relatively rapidly, some pesticide residues may remain on the surface of or in grass blades for a few days or even a few weeks. Therefore, collected clippings may have pesticide residues.

Factors that cause degradation of pesticides in clippings (thatch and soil):

- Microbial activity
  Most pesticides are organic compounds that bacteria and other microorganisms use for food.
- Ultraviolet light
  Pesticides that remain near the surface may be degraded by sunlight.
- Chemical degradation

To *minimize* risk from pesticides in clippings:

- Use pesticides without a long residual.
- Consider pesticide residues, especially herbicides, before using clippings for mulch or compost.

Effects on Non-Target Organisms

Important organisms that occur naturally in turfgrass and may be affected by pesticide applications include:

- Beneficial insects and other arthropods
- Earthworms
- Fungi and other microorganisms that compete with pathogens
- Fungi and other microorganisms that degrade thatch

To *minimize* risk to non-target organisms:

- Use pesticides only when necessary.
- Spot-treat only infested areas.
- Use relatively specific pesticides which affect pests but not beneficial organisms.

Toxicity to Humans and Other Vertebrates

Toxicity and other health risks of pesticides vary considerably between types of pesticides. Insecticides and nematicides tend to be the most toxic to vertebrate animals because most are nerve poisons. Fungicides and herbicides are generally less acutely toxic than insecticides and nematicides, but may have other health risks.

To *minimize* risk to humans and other vertebrates:

- Use pesticides only when necessary.
- Spot-treat only infested areas.
- Provide appropriate protective equipment for the applicator.
- Choose less toxic pesticides whenever possible.
- Time applications to reduce exposure to golfers, animals, and other non-target organisms (e.g., honeybees).

Mixing and Handling Considerations

Pesticide exposure and/or spills can occur during:

- Mixing   • Loading   • Storage

To *minimize* risks during mixing and handling:

- Mix away from wells and surface water.
- Mix away from general public access.

- Use a proper containment facility to handle spills.
- Store pesticides properly and according to all regulations. (sturdy shelving, supplies to contain small spills)

Technical Data Sheets

In addition to pesticide labels and material safety data sheets (MSDS), chemical companies can provide you with a "technical data sheet" or "technical bulletin" upon request. These sheets/bulletins provide useful information about the product, especially in regard to environmental risks. In some parts of the country, information in these sheets/bulletins is required for development of IPM plans, water protection plans, and other proposals.

TIMING OF APPLICATION FOR OPTIMAL EFFECT

Each turf pest or pathogen has its own life cycle or period of development. There are times when the pest or pathogen is more vulnerable to chemical control. Some pesticides do not remain active for a long period of time, so timing of application of these materials must be very precise. Other materials remain active longer (residual).

Example: If a superintendent finds large grubs in the soil, he should use a fast-acting insecticide to manage these grubs quickly, before they cause more damage. If grubs are still very small, a slower but longer-lasting insecticide might be more appropriate.

Example: Certain fungicides may protect roots from invasion by fungi that cause root diseases (e.g., necrotic ring spot, Pythium root rot, summer patch, take-all patch). If a superintendent waits until disease symptoms occur, it means that the disease has developed to the point where the roots are so badly infected that the leaf blades are affected. Application of a fungicide at that time is not likely to provide good results because considerable damage has already occurred. In addition, diseased roots are not likely to absorb much fungicide (Figure 6.3).

Example: Pre-emergence herbicides for crabgrass are not effective once the seeds have germinated and the plants are established.

Pesticide applications may be any of the following types:

Figure 6.3. Diseased roots on left; healthy on right. (Courtesy M.L. Elliott.)

Figure 6.4. Applying pesticides (Nashawtuc Country Club, Concord, Massachusetts). (Courtesy P.J. Vittum.)

Preventive

Preventive applications are applied before turf damage is obvious.

Disadvantage:

Application is made before the extent of damage is known, so some areas may be treated unnecessarily.

Curative

Curative applications are applied after symptom or injury has occurred.

Disadvantage:

Even if the pesticide is effective, some recovery time will be necessary for the turf; the application may be too late to be effective.

Examples

Insects — Some insecticides kill the target insect within 1 to 3 days (curative), while others require 2 to 3 weeks (may be preventive or curative).

Diseases — Preventive fungicide applications are most effective for root and crown diseases; both preventive and curative applications may be used for many foliar diseases.

Weeds — Preventive: pre-emergence herbicides.
                Curative: post-emergence herbicides

Timing of pre-emergence herbicides is critical because applications made too early or too late will give unsatisfactory results. Post-emergence herbicides are more effective on seedlings than on mature plants.

> All turf management personnel are trained to identify common symptoms associated with turfgrass pests. The combination of daily scouting and proper turf management practices enables us to use a curative management program, thus limiting the amount of plant protectants applied on the golf course.
>
> — John Vance Much, Golf Course Superintendent, Semiahmoo Golf and Country Club, Blaine, Washington

CHARACTERISTICS OF THE PESTICIDE

Several physical and chemical characteristics should be considered when selecting a pesticide.

Speed of Efficacy

Some pesticides begin to work within a few hours or a day after application, while others may take 2 or 3 weeks to begin to affect the target pest.

Figure 6.5. Pesticide sprayer. (Courtesy P.P. Cobb.)

Residual Activity

Some pesticides will only remain active for 1 to 2 weeks, while others may remain active for 2 or 3 months. Usually short-lived insecticides should not be used too early in an insect's life cycle because the material may break down before all of the insects hatch. Conversely, a long-lasting insecticide may not control a destructive insect pest population quickly enough, so additional damage may occur before the insecticide takes effect.

Protectant fungicides which coat the leaf blade will vary in their residual activity depending on rainfall and plant growth. Turf cannot be seeded or sodded until the residual of certain herbicides is gone. Read labels carefully if you need to renovate areas after construction, winter injury, or other turf problems.

Insecticides:	Active Period
some pyrethroids, some organophosphates	7–10 days
some pyrethroids, most organophosphates, most carbamates	2–5 weeks
imidacloprid (Merit)	more than 6 weeks
fipronil (Choice)	more than 3 months

Fungicides:	Active Period
contact/protectants	7–14 days
localized penetrant/systemics	14–21 days
systemics	21–28 days

Herbicides:	Active Period
pre-emergence herbicides	6-12 weeks
post-emergence herbicides	10-14 days

Figure 6.6. Covered boom sprayer. (Courtesy F.D. Dinelli.)

Formulation

Granules can be applied dry with a spreader.

Sprayable Formulations:

- Wettable and soluble powders
- Emulsifiable concentrates
- Flowables
- Dry flowables
- Water dispersible granules

Factors in Choices:

- Ease of handling
- Phytotoxicity
- Residual activity
- Storage needs

- Exposure to applicator
- Speed of efficacy
- Cost
- Available application equipment

WATER QUALITY AND AMOUNTS REQUIRED

Some pesticides break down very rapidly in alkaline water (water with pH above 8.0 to 8.5). If the water supply used for pesticide applications has a high pH, an additive (buffer, acidifier) should be used to lower or stabilize the water. An extreme example is trichlorfon (Proxol or Dylox), which can break down to an inactive form in less than two hours if the tank water has a pH of 9.0 or more.

Some pesticides must be watered in immediately *after* application. In other situations, an area should be irrigated 24 to 36 hours *before* application to increase effectiveness. For example, to control mole crickets or white grubs when the soil is extremely dry, it is necessary to irrigate so these insects will move closer to the surface where the insecticide will be located. See label directions for specific recommendations. The following general recommendations apply:

Insecticides/Nematicides

Most insecticides should be watered in to some degree shortly after application, in part to reduce surface exposure. Some insecticides, including many directed toward soil insects, should be watered in heavily (0.25 to 0.5 inch, 0.6–1.27 cm) immediately after application. Others, including many directed toward surface-feeding insects, should be watered in very lightly. Use of acephate is an exception.

Fungicides

Fungicides applied to control leaf diseases should be allowed to dry before irrigation or rainfall. Fungicides applied to control root diseases may need to be watered in to move the product to the root zone.

Herbicides

A few products require irrigation after application. Many require contact with the plant tissue to be effective.

SPECTRUM OF ACTIVITY

Insecticides Used to Reduce Insect Populations

Most traditional insecticides currently on the turf market are "broad spectrum" materials, and will be at least somewhat detrimental to most kinds of insects with which they come in contact, including many beneficial insects, such as predatory beetles. However, properties of the products (mobility, tendency to adsorb to organic matter) will determine how much contact actually occurs.

Example: Chlorpyrifos (Dursban) is adsorbed in the thatch very quickly and does not penetrate into soil below established turfgrass nearly as well as some other products. Therefore, it would be less effective against soil insects, such as white grubs, but also less detrimental to some of the beneficial soil organisms.

Figure 6.7. Replacing sprayer nozzles. Proper maintenance assures uniformity and correct application rates. (Courtesy P.P. Cobb.)

Some products are markedly more effective against certain kinds of insects.

Example: Carbaryl (Sevin) tends to be very effective against caterpillars, whether on turf or in ornamental plantings.

(See Chapter 7 for further information.)

Fungicides Used to Prevent or Reduce Diseases Caused by Fungi

These chemicals will temporarily suppress pathogen populations, but do not eliminate them. If disease-conducive conditions continue, disease will recur as soon as the fungicide control interval has passed.

It is important to read fungicide labels carefully, because a single fungicide will not control all diseases. Some are fairly broad spectrum; others are quite specific. For instance, metalaxyl is effective against *Pythium* diseases but is not useful for other common turf diseases such as dollar spot and brown patch.

Some fungicides enter plant tissue and provide some curative action against fungi that have already infected the plant. No fungicide will bring dead plants back to life.

(See Chapter 8 for further information.)

Nematicides Used to Reduce Nematode Populations

Most nematicides are restricted-use pesticides because they are extremely toxic (to people and other vertebrates). In addition, many nematicides are very

Figure 6.8. Spot-treating mole cricket tunnels at Olde Florida Golf Club, Naples, Florida. (Courtesy D. Davis.)

toxic to insects, including numerous beneficial parasites and predators. As a result, the natural control normally provided by these beneficial insects is lost. Nematicides should be applied only when a laboratory nematode assay confirms that nematodes exceed established local damage thresholds.

(See Chapter 9 for further information.)

Herbicides Used to Reduce Weed Populations

Herbicides are generally classified based on when they are applied (pre-emergence vs. post-emergence) and by their spectrum of activity (selective vs. nonselective). Selective herbicides normally are effective on some plants but are not effective on other kinds of plants. Generally, the selectivity is based on whether the target weed is a grassy weed (e.g., goosegrass, crabgrass), a broad-leaf weed (e.g., dandelion, clover), or a sedge (e.g., nutsedge).

It is important to know the tolerance of your turf to certain selective herbicides, particularly the ones used to control grassy weeds. Labels may include Latin names or common names of plants, but common names of plants vary from one region of the country to another, and may be confusing. Check with your local specialists before using new or unfamiliar products.

(See Chapter 10 for further information.)

RESISTANCE MANAGEMENT

The mode of action of a pesticide describes how it acts against its target pest or pathogen. When the same pesticide is used repeatedly, its effectiveness may be reduced. This may result in "resistance" or "tolerance" in the pest or pathogen population. If pesticides with the same mode of action are used repeatedly, it is as though you used the same pesticide every time. Therefore, it is important to mix or alternate pesticides with different modes of action during the course of a season and from year to year. More detailed information is available in Chapters 7, 8, 9, and 10.

SENSITIVITY TO MICROBIAL DEGRADATION

Some pesticides are broken down readily by microbes living in the soil or the thatch. When a pesticide is applied, the microbes that degrade it will multiply. If the pesticide is applied repeatedly, these microbes may build up in sufficient numbers to render additional applications virtually useless. This phenomenon is known as "enhanced degradation" and can appear to be resistance. Enhanced degradation of isofenphos (Oftanol) is a familiar example for many golf course superintendents, particularly in the central part of the country. This problem has also occurred following repeated use of certain fungicides, herbicides, and nematicides.

STATE AND LOCAL REGULATIONS

Every pesticide used in the United States must be registered by the federal Environmental Protection Agency (EPA). In addition, pesticides must be registered for use in each individual state. States always have the option of making their registration requirements stricter than the federal label. For example, a state may disallow use in particular counties because sensitive soil types or endangered species are present, or it may specifically prohibit use of a product within a specified distance of surface water or wellheads.

FURTHER READING

Balogh, J.C. and J.L. Anderson. Environmental Impacts of Turfgrass Pesticides, in *Golf Course Management and Construction*. Balogh, J.C. and W.J. Walker, Eds., Lewis Publishers, Boca Raton, FL, 1992.

Cohen, S.Z. Agriculture and the Golf Course Industry: An Exploration of Pesticide Use. *Golf Course Management*. 63(5):96,100,102,104, 1995.

Cooper, R.J. Evaluating the Run-Off and Leaching Potential of Turfgrass Pesticides. *Golf Course Management*. 58(2):8–16, 1990.

Croke, S. Weather Forecasting and Chemical Application. *Golf Course Management*. 62(2):136–139, 1994.

Gaussoin, R. Pesticide Formulations. *Golf Course Management*. 63(3):49–51, 1995.

Hull, R.J. The fate of pesticides used on turf. *TurfGrass Trends*. 4(9):2–11, 1995.

Johnson, B.J. Reduced herbicide application rates: crabgrass and goosegrass control in bermudagrass. *TurfGrass Trends.* 5(1):1–6, 1996.

Kenna, M.P. What Happens to Pesticides Applied to Golf Courses? *USGA Green Section Record.* 33(1):1–9, 1995.

Hurdzan, M.J. Minimizing Environmental Impact by Golf Course Development: A Method and Some Case Studies, in *Handbook of Integrated Pest Management for Turf and Ornamentals*, Leslie, A.R., Ed., Lewis Publishers, Boca Raton, FL, 1994.

Linde, D.T., T.L. Watschke, and J.A. Borger. Tracking Turf Runoff. *Grounds Maintenance.* 31(3):18,20,22,24, 1996.

Murphy, T.R. Herbicide-resistant weeds in turfgrasses. *TurfGrass Trends.* 5(1):7–10, 1996.

Nelson, E.B. Maximizing Disease Control with Fungicide Applications: The Basics of Turfgrass Fungicides. *TurfGrass Trends:* Part One: Fungicide Use and General Properties. 5(2):10–17, 1996. Part Two: Behavior in Soil. 5(3):5–11, 1996. Part Three: Plant and Pathogen Factors Affecting Fungicide Efficacy. 5(4):1–7, 1996. Part Four: Handling and Applying Fungicides. 5(8):10–15, 1996. Part Five: Record Keeping. 5(12):1–5, 1996. Part Six: Human Health and Environmental Quality Considerations. 5(12):15–18, 1996.

Petrovic, A.M., N.R. Borromeo, and M.J. Carroll. Fate of Pesticides in the Turfgrass Environment, in *Handbook of Integrated Pest Management for Turf and Ornamentals*, Leslie, A.R., Ed., Lewis Publishers, Boca Raton, FL, 1994.

Smith, A.E. Turf Pesticide Mobility in Soil. *Grounds Maintenance.* 31(3):14–17, 1996.

Soloman, K.R., S.A. Harris, and G.R. Stephenson. Pesticide Exposure: What is the Risk? *Grounds Maintenance.* 27(3):60,62,110, 1992.

Villani, M.G. Relationships among soil insects, soil insecticides, and soil physical properties. *TurfGrass Trends.* 4(9):11–17, 1995.

Vittum, P.J. Back to Basics—Insecticide Primer. *TurfGrass Trends.* Part One: What Insecticides Can and Cannot Do. 5(8):1–8, 1996. Part Two: Chemical Classes of Turfgrass Insecticides. 6(1):9–17, 1997. Part Three: Insecticide Formulations. 6(4):1–8, 1997.

CHAPTER **7**

PEST MANAGEMENT: INSECTS

GENERAL BIOLOGY

Numerous insects can be found in or on turf. Some of these insects cause damage directly or indirectly to the turf, while others are beneficial (e.g., parasites or predators of pests, or active in breaking down thatch). Damage that appears as a result of insect activity may resemble certain diseases (off-color patches which spread over time), drought stress, or even rototilling.

A few basic concepts about insect biology are helpful in identifying insects, understanding their life cycles, predicting their activity, and determining appropriate control options.

Metamorphosis

Most insects begin as eggs, which hatch into small immature insects. These immature forms go through a series of molts, gradually increasing in size, and finally develop into adults. This developmental process is called metamorphosis, which means "change."

Incomplete or Gradual Metamorphosis

Immature insects closely resemble the adults, except that they lack wings. All stages feed on the same food sources, so immatures (nymphs) and adults compete for food.

> *Examples:* aphids, chinch bugs, cockroaches, grasshoppers, mole crickets (Figure 7.1)

Complete Metamorphosis

Immature insects bear no resemblance to the adult. There is an additional developmental stage (the pupa), during which the insect is transformed from the larva (immature) to the adult. Often the larvae feed on different kinds of food than the adults, so they are not in direct competition.

> *Examples:* white grubs (Figure 7.2) to beetles, caterpillars to moths, maggots to flies

Figure 7.1. Mole cricket life stages. (Courtesy P.P. Cobb.)

Mouth Parts

Insects have several different ways of obtaining food. The most common kinds of mouth parts in turf insects are:

Chewing

Heavily armored mandibles are used to chew food laterally. (The mouth-parts move from side to side rather than up and down.) Plant tissue is eaten directly, so stems or roots may be severed or leaves may have numerous holes.

Examples: mole crickets, caterpillars, white grubs

Piercing/Sucking

A special hypodermic needle-like structure is inserted into the plant and used to suck juices out of the plant. Plant tissue is not removed directly, but may turn yellow overall and have a blotchy appearance.

Examples: aphids, chinch bugs, greenbugs, ground pearls, spittlebugs

Life Cycles

An insect species may complete one to several generations per year — or may take several years to complete one generation. Each species has its own "normal" cycle, so in most years it will complete the same number of generations. In cold, temperate climates, insects must be able to survive winter conditions or migrate in each year from milder climates. Some species survive best as adults; others survive as eggs or immatures.

Figure 7.2. White grubs. (Courtesy P.J. Vittum.)

Examples

Mole Crickets: one generation per year in most areas; two generations per year in south Florida, and they normally spend the winter as large nymphs or adults.

White Grubs: most species have one generation per year and overwinter as grubs; some species (e.g., May beetles) take two or three years to complete one generation in the northern United States.

KEY STEPS IN INSECT MANAGEMENT

Identify the Insect

Distinguishing characteristics on an insect are often fairly easy to see, especially with a hand lens or dissecting microscope. Some of the insect characteristics an IPM scout should be able to recognize are:

- What stage of development?
  - larva?
  - nymph?
  - pupa?
  - adult?
- Does it have wings? How many?
- Does it have legs?
- Where in the turf does it occur (surface? thatch? root zone?)
- How big is it?
- Color patterns (Does it have a brown head and white body? Is it brown all over? Does it have stripes or spots or tufts or scales?)

- What kind of damage is associated with it?
  - discrete off-color patches?
  - general drought-like stress?
  - turf pulls up in tufts?
  - roots destroyed?
- Where does the damage occur? (Figure 7.3)
  - edges of fairways? (Figure 7.4)
  - one grass species only?
  - sandy soils?
  - sunny areas?
- When is it active?
  - time of day?
  - time of year?

How to Get Help with Insect Identifications

Establish a good working relationship with your state Extension service or with a reputable commercial consultant. While most turf insects are large enough for a well-trained person to be able to identify, inevitably you will encounter an insect pest you have never seen before. Be able to describe the most important features (see the list above) to a specialist, and be prepared to collect a sample to send to a laboratory for confirmation of an identification.

How to Collect and Ship an Insect Sample

1. If possible, collect several specimens from the damaged area.
    Hard-bodied insects (e.g., mole crickets, beetles)
    - Transfer to a small container of rubbing alcohol, which will preserve them for a few days.

    Soft-bodied insects (e.g., caterpillars)
    - Send live specimens in a core (3 to 4 inches [10 to 12 cm] in diameter) of turf

    – or –

    - Blanch the insects (boil for 10 to 20 seconds) and then transfer them to rubbing alcohol

    Be sure that any samples containing rubbing alcohol are well-sealed!

2. Deliver specimens directly to the diagnostic laboratory or mail them First Class. Do NOT mail on a Friday or Saturday! Note that it may be best to use an overnight delivery service because most universities have a large receiving department, and packages may take several days to arrive at the lab.

3. Include a thorough description of the problem, including:
    - Symptoms
    - What grass species are affected

Figure 7.3. White grub damage on a fairway. (Courtesy P.J. Vittum.)

Figure 7.4. Annual bluegrass weevil damage on the edge of a fairway. (Courtesy P.J. Vittum.)

- What mowing height areas are affected (roughs, fairways, tees, or greens)
- Pattern of occurrence (all over? shady areas only? low lying areas only?)
- Date when problem was first noticed?
- Any pesticides or fertilizers applied to the area in the past three weeks?

4. Include your name, telephone number, and address so the diagnostician can contact you once a diagnosis has been made or ask additional questions.

Know How Often to Scout

The frequency of sampling for insect pests depends on:

- **Species of insect involved and its potential for damage.**
  An insect with the potential to cause serious damage in a short period of time should be monitored much more frequently than a minor pest.

- **Stage of development.**
  White grubs should be monitored more frequently when they are in the first or second instar (immature stage). This is when they are large enough to be observed, but still small enough to be vulnerable to control.
  Mole crickets should be monitored more frequently (using a soapy flush) as adults begin to lay eggs and as eggs begin to hatch. Many insecticides are markedly more effective when directed toward very young nymphs, therefore first or peak hatch must be determined by monitoring.

- **Weather conditions.**
  Extreme conditions will increase stress on the turf so it cannot tolerate as much pest activity.

- **Curative control options available.**
  If curative options (i.e., ones that will work even after an insect population becomes active) are not available, scouting must be done very frequently and the first sign of insect activity may require a management decision.

- **Tournament Schedules**
  If you expect a pest problem to coincide with a scheduled tournament, increase the frequency of sampling.

> Timing insecticide treatments to control young, more vulnerable mole crickets is the key to control. I monitor first and peak hatch in the spring, and time treatments accordingly. With short-residual insecticides, monitoring enables me to wait as long as possible to treat, giving a larger "window of opportunity." This results in excellent control that is cost-effective.
>
> — Jeffrey P. Cornelson, CGCS, Azalea City Golf Course, Mobile, Alabama

Understand the Life Cycle

As a general rule, insects are very difficult to control in the egg and pupal stages. For most turf insects, control efforts should be directed at immature stages or (in a few instances) adults. It is a waste of money (and chemicals and time) to try to control an insect when the pest is not vulnerable to control. If the life cycle is well understood, control strategies can be selected and applied in a manner to maximize their effectiveness.

Monitoring should be carried out at the right time of year, in the right locations (where the insects are active), and looking for the right stages of the insect (Figure 7.5).

> *Example:* During the summer months, Japanese beetle adults will be flying during the daytime and feeding on numerous flowering trees and shrubs. Scouting should include the use of pheromone traps to determine when flights begin and when they peak. The grubs (immature stage in the turf root zone), however, will not be present in large numbers for about four weeks after adults first become visible, so scouting for grubs should be suspended until that time.

ENVIRONMENTAL FACTORS THAT AFFECT INSECT DEVELOPMENT

Air and Soil Temperatures

Most insects have optimum temperatures at which they develop most rapidly. When air or soil temperatures are markedly higher or lower than that optimum temperature, insect development can be slowed or stopped. Usually, higher temperatures increase the rate of development, so unusually warm springs often lead to fast development of insects from one stage to the next.

Figure 7.5. Monitoring for grubs. (Courtesy P.J. Vittum.)

Soil Type

This can affect insect movement or development. Many soil insects (e.g., mole crickets) are much more mobile or active in sandy soils than in clayey soils. Some insects (e.g., black turfgrass ataenius) prefer soils with slightly higher levels of organic matter.

Soil Moisture

Many insect eggs (e.g., white grubs) are laid in soil and are subject to desiccation if soil is too dry. Insect eggs will suffocate if soils are too wet, but often must be submerged for several days before they die.

Thatch

Thatch thickness and density can affect development of some turf insects. Chinch bugs and some other surface-active insects thrive in thick thatch.

Weather Fronts

Several insects overwinter in areas south of (and warmer than) the point of infestation. In the spring, as temperatures increase, the adults are caught in weather fronts and are blown hundreds of miles north, back to the areas they will infest. Superintendents can learn to predict when black cutworms will return to an area by monitoring weather patterns in the spring.

Day Length

In some cases, insect activity is triggered by day length. Insects can detect light vs. dark, and many insects begin their spring development as day length begins to increase. Similarly, many insects begin to prepare for winter (slow their metabolism, look for protected sites) as day length begins to decrease.

Develop a pest profile for each insect pest! (See Chapter 2)

CULTURAL CONTROL STRATEGIES

Selection of Turfgrass Species and/or Cultivars

The annual bluegrass weevil feeds primarily on annual bluegrass. In areas where this weevil is a serious problem, concentrate on converting the annual bluegrass to another grass species.

Some cultivars of perennial ryegrass and fescue have endophytes (Chapter 5), which render them resistant to (or at least more tolerant of) several thatch or surface-active insects, such as cutworms, webworms, chinch bugs, and billbugs.

If it is not possible to renovate or replace an inappropriate turfgrass species or cultivar, then even more care should be taken to provide the optimal agronomic conditions for that turf. In this way, some stresses can be reduced.

Mowing Heights

As noted in Chapter 4, mowing is one cultural practice that has a direct bearing on the overall vigor of the turfgrass. Each turfgrass species has a range of heights within which it grows best.

- Turfgrasses that are mowed below the optimum height will be stressed and less able to withstand insect activity.
- Raise the height of cut where possible. Insect populations may still be present but the damage they cause will usually be less severe and less noticeable at higher cuts.
- If necessary, incorporate other cultural techniques to compensate for the higher mowing height:
  - double cut greens or collars
  - use rollers (Figure 7.6)
  - topdress
  - vertical cutting
- Explain to the golfers, the greens committee, the golf professional, and any other appropriate audience why you are raising the mowing height on certain parts of the golf course. Include information on the economic and environmental cost of using more pesticides (insecticides, fungicides, herbicides) to maintain the golf course at lower mowing heights.

Example: The annual bluegrass weevil (Hyperodes weevil) only damages annual bluegrass at fairway heights or lower. While weevils do occur in neighboring roughs, damage has never been observed at the higher cuts. There is evidence that raising the height of the putting green or collar enables it to recover more quickly from weevil damage.

Irrigation Strategies

Irrigation is an essential cultural tool used to provide adequate moisture to the root zone and to provide evaporational cooling. Many turf insects are quite mobile, and will migrate from one location to another over time. Sometimes

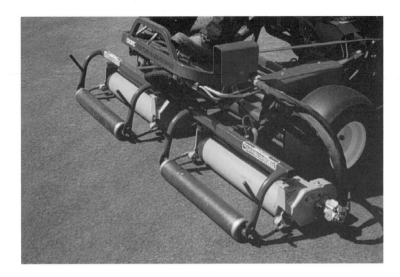

Figure 7.6. Green rollers help avoid low mowing. (Courtesy F.D. Dinelli.)

soil or thatch moisture is a driving force in their movement. In other words, if soil (or thatch) is too dry, the insects will move laterally in search of a more "friendly" environment or downward in the soil profile to get away from the dry conditions or high temperatures.

Some insect activity can be masked by irrigating the affected area. While the insect population will not be affected (the numbers may remain the same), the turfgrass will be able to recover more quickly from insect damage.

> *Example:* The damage caused by hairy chinch bugs feeding on cool season turfgrasses can be masked by providing adequate irrigation for the turf.

In extremely dry conditions, some insects (e.g., mole crickets and some white grubs) will migrate down through the soil profile to escape the high temperatures. If you try to apply an insecticide at this time, the material will not penetrate far enough into the root zone to contact the target insects. Irrigation of the area to be treated about 24 to 36 hours *before* making an insecticide application will cause the insects to move back into the root zone and greatly improve the effectiveness of the insecticide application. (See also discussion in Chapter 4.)

Thatch Management

Some insects (e.g., chinch bugs, some caterpillars) thrive in thick thatch conditions (>1 inch, 2.54 cm) and can be put at a competitive disadvantage by dethatching. Very thick and/or dense thatch can also make it difficult for water to penetrate to the soil zone. In these conditions, the turf roots will be under

Figure 7.7. Core aeration. (Courtesy P.J. Vittum.)

added stress and will be more vulnerable to attack from soil insects such as white grubs. (See also discussion in Chapter 4.)

BIOLOGICAL CONTROL STRATEGIES

Several biological control options are available for use on turf insects. These are discussed in some detail in Chapter 5. Incorporating biological control into a traditional insect control program is sometimes challenging because some biological control agents are susceptible to the traditional insecticides that also may be used. (Table 7.1)

Successful Use of Biocontrol Agents

Parasites — are not currently available commercially for use on turf, but often occur naturally. Most insect parasites are adversely affected by broad-spectrum insecticides.

Predators — are not currently available commercially for use on turf, but often occur naturally. Most insect predators are adversely affected by broad-spectrum insecticides.

Entomopathogenic Nematodes — should be applied early in the morning or in the evening to reduce the rate of desiccation. Water-in the nematodes immediately after application. Check the label for compatibility with traditional insecticides (whether in tank mixes or in followup applications). Use *coarse* filters — or remove the filters altogether. Apply when the target insect is in the

Figure 7.8. Weeds encroach where turf is damaged by mole crickets. (Courtesy P.P. Cobb.)

most susceptible stage of development. Some nematodes kill the target insects within a few days, while others take longer to begin to work.

Bacteria — appear to be somewhat less sensitive to desiccation than nematodes, but some may be sensitive to breakdown in sunlight. Follow label directions regarding post-application watering. Apply when the target insect is in the smallest stages of development. Some bacteria or bacterial products (e.g., BT) paralyze the gut of the target insect within a few days, so feeding ceases. The insect may not die as quickly as it does when subjected to a traditional insecticide.

Fungi — are just becoming available commercially. Some formulations may be sensitive to breakdown in sunlight. Follow label directions for application.

Endophytes — are already present in endophyte seed and will continue to function for the life of the plant. They are available in some cultivars of perennial ryegrass and some fescues.

Insect Growth Regulators (IGR) — can normally be applied in the same manner as traditional insecticides, but must be targeted to the stages of development of the insect that are sensitive to the IGR. Most IGRs are most effective when directed toward young immatures.

When it comes to insects, e.g., white grubs, chart out the areas that sustained damage during the previous season. Follow up with a scouting process that includes evidence of beetles flying around during the mating season and damage done to linden trees, for example, and susceptible ornamentals. Then visit the affected sites to establish a per-square-foot count. At this point the degree of treatment needed will be established by taking into consideration areas that we wish to prioritize because of their importance, i.e., greens, tees, fairways, and roughs, treating the smallest possible acreage at all times.

Similarly, the same procedure is followed for Hyperodes weevils. After the first timely spring application, we are able to control the little pests by monitoring their activity and treating the collars of greens, which seem to be most susceptible. We spot-treat fairway perimeters.

IPM practices, taken seriously, are a means of assessing an entire management scheme and making concessions for cultural practices such as aeration, reduction of nitrogen and water applications, creating air movement, etc., to reduce the use of pesticides. A simple question one must ask oneself when following an IPM program is, "How can I do my job well using all the resources available to me, leaving pesticide usage for last?"

— Robert U. Alonzi, CGCS, Winged Foot Golf Club, Mamaroneck, New York

Table 7.1. Biocontrols for insects.

Biocontrol Agent	Target Insect	Commercial Examples
Entomopathogenic Nematodes		
Steinernema carpocapsae	caterpillars, billbug	BioSafe, Vector
Steinernema glaseri	white grubs	(not yet available)
Steinernema riobravis	mole cricket	Vector MC
Steinernema scapterisci	mole cricket	Proactant
Heterorhabditis bacteriophora	white grubs, billbugs	Cruiser
Bacteria/Bacterial Products		
Bacillus thuringiensis		
var. *japonensis* (*buibui* strain)	white grubs	(not yet available)
var. *israelensis*	mosquitoes	Bactimos, Technar, Vectobac
var. *kurstaki*	caterpillars	Dipel, Steward, Javelin
Bacillus popilliae	Japanese beetle grubs	Doom, Japidemic
Fungi		
Beauvaria bassiana	chinch bug, billbug	(not yet available)
Metarhizium anisopliae	white grubs	(not yet available)

CHEMICAL CONTROL STRATEGIES

Chemical control of turf insect pests is carried out by applying chemical insecticides. While some environmental activists are reluctant to recognize that insecticides and other pesticides have a place in an IPM program, they are indeed one of many tools in the program. Keep in mind, however, that using an insecticide is a way of treating the symptom (the insect population), but it does not necessarily deal with the cause (Why are the insects there in the first place?). In an aggressive IPM program, the superintendent will try to determine why the insect problem has occurred, look for cultural strategies that can be used to reduce turf stress or reduce insect populations, consider any biological control options that are available, and then use insecticides in areas where scouting has indicated that populations are high enough to warrant their use.

As with most pesticides, insecticides are limited in what they can and cannot do. Factors to consider include:

Efficacy — Insecticides usually will not eliminate every pest insect. There will be a few survivors. Some insecticides are more effective than others. The challenge is to reduce the population to a tolerable level.

Resistance Problems — Overuse or misapplication of an insecticide may lead to the development of individuals that are resistant to the material, and who, in turn, pass on their "successful" genes to the next generation, ultimately leading to the development of a population of insects that is unaffected by that insecticide.

Application Requirements — Some insecticides require watering-in before or after application, while others do not. Failure to follow directions on the label can lead to failure of the insecticide to suppress the insect population.

Thatch Effects — Some insecticides can penetrate thatch more readily than others. In general, use a material that can penetrate thatch for soil insects (e.g., white grubs, mole crickets) and use a material that is bound to the thatch for thatch feeders (e.g., cutworms, armyworms). Ask a university specialist which materials would be appropriate.

Local Conditions — Insecticide use patterns vary from one region of the country to another because certain insecticides are not as effective in some locations. Base your final insecticide decisions on local research and local recommendations.

> *Example:* Insecticides that are very sensitive to high pH (such as acephate, isazofos, or trichlorfon) should not be used in areas where the water supply has a high pH (8.5 or higher) unless a tank additive is included to buffer the mix.

Non-Target Effects — Remember that most turf insecticides are "broad-spectrum" materials and can have a detrimental effect on beneficial arthropods, such as naturally occurring predatory beetles, spiders, and parasitic wasps. Avoid using insecticides when beneficial insects are particularly active.

Types of Insecticides

Contact Insecticides

Most insecticides must come in direct physical contact with the target insect to be effective. This most often occurs when turf is treated and then an insect walks or crawls through the treated area. The residue of the insecticide comes in contact with the cuticle (outer covering) of the insect and penetrates into the internal tissue. Most contact insecticides interfere with the insect nervous system at some level. Besides penetrating through the cuticle, the target insect may ingest some of a contact insecticide into the digestive system, from which it is absorbed into the bloodstream and ultimately reaches the nervous system.

The term "contact" also refers to insecticides that remain on the treated surface of a plant and are not absorbed into the internal plant tissues.

Systemic Insecticides

Some turf insecticides are absorbed into the internal tissue of a treated plant and move within the vascular tissue of that plant to other locations. Insects which then feed on the plant ingest the insecticide, either by feeding near the original point of application or by sucking plant juices elsewhere on the plant.

Stomach Poison Insecticides

Some insecticides must be ingested by the target insect and are then absorbed through the gut wall into the internal tissue. They may be nerve poisons or they may interfere with the digestive process, but in either case they cannot penetrate the insect cuticle directly.

Characteristics of Insecticides

Fast-acting and short-lived insecticides

- Have a noticeable effect on the target insect within *1 to 3 days* after application.
- Tend to breakdown to an inactive form within *2 weeks.*

Figure 7.9. Insecticide test plots for grub control. (Courtesy P.J. Vittum.)

- Are usually very soluble in water and therefore have the greatest risk of runoff or leaching.

Examples: acephate, trichlorfon

Medium-speed and residual insecticides

- Have a noticeable effect on the target insect within *3 to 7 days* after application.
- Usually remain active for *2 to 5 weeks* (depending on temperature and moisture conditions).
- Mobility in soil is highly variable. Some are quite mobile, while others are relatively immobile; some are tied up in organic matter (e.g., thatch), while others pass through thatch fairly readily.

Examples: bendiocarb, chlorpyrifos, ethoprop

Slow-acting and long-lived insecticides

- Often take *10 to 20 days* to have a noticeable effect on the target insect.
- Tend to remain active for *6 or more weeks.*
- Are usually less mobile than the fast-acting compounds, but because of their persistence, they still can be subject to leaching or runoff.

Examples: fipronil, imidacloprid, isofenphos

Chemical Classes of Insecticides

Turf insecticides can be classified according to their chemical structure. Most of these materials are "organic" in that they contain carbon, hydrogen, and oxygen somewhere in the molecule. Each chemical class has a feature particular to the structure.

Carbamates

- Are derivatives of carbamic acid and have a nitrogen atom and two oxygen atoms attached to the same carbon atom.
- Have a range of toxicities to mammals and other vertebrates. (Some are relatively low in acute toxicity, and others are extremely toxic.)
- Usually do not accumulate in the food chain.
- Some are quite persistent in soil, while others break down very quickly.
- Some are virtually insoluble, and therefore quite immobile, while others are extremely mobile in water.
- Tend to be quite toxic to earthworms as well as some non-target arthropods.

Examples: bendiocarb, carbaryl

Chloronicotinyls

- Have several nitrogen atoms and one or more ring structures in the molecule.
- Are relatively low in acute toxicity to mammals and most other vertebrates.
- Do not accumulate in the food chain.
- Are quite persistent in soil.
- Are somewhat mobile and, so, sometimes run off to surface water, but break down quickly in standing water.
- Appear not to be disruptive to several beneficial insects and other arthropods.

Example: imidacloprid

Organophosphates

- Have the element phosphorus in the molecule (double-bonded to oxygen or sulfur).
- Have a range of toxicities to mammals and other vertebrates. (Some are relatively low in acute toxicity, and others are extremely toxic.)
- Usually do not accumulate in the food chain.

- Some are quite persistent in the soil, while others break down very quickly.
- Some are virtually insoluble and, therefore, quite immobile, while others are extremely mobile in water.
- Often are broad-spectrum in activity, and therefore have harmful effects on non-target insects and other arthropods.

Examples: acephate, chlorpyrifos, ethoprop, fonofos, isazofos, isofenphos, trichlorfon

Phenylpyrazoles

- Have fluorine, chlorine, and several nitrogen atoms in the molecule.
- Are moderately toxic following exposure to a single dose.
- Apparently do not accumulate in the food chain.
- Are quite persistent in the soil.
- Are quite immobile in the soil.
- Appear not to be disruptive to several beneficial insects and other arthropods.

Example: fipronil

Synthetic Pyrethroids

- Are based on the structure of pyrethrum, a natural product that occurs in some chrysanthemums. Scientists have experimented with the shape of the molecule to enhance the performance of the material.
- Are usually relatively low in acute toxicity to mammals but often are quite toxic to fish.
- Vary in their persistence in field conditions.
- Do not accumulate in the food chain.
- May be sensitive to breakdown in sunlight.
- Vary in their solubility and mobility in water.

Examples: bifenthrin, lambda-cyhalothrin, cyfluthrin

Selecting an Insecticide

If you determine that an insecticide must be used to reduce a pest insect population, consider several factors before deciding which material to use: (Table 7.2)

Local recommendations: Has the material been tested and recommended in your state or region?

Table 7.2. Characteristics of some turf insecticides.

Common Name	Trade Name[1]	Chemical Class	Speed[2]	Residual[3]
acephate	Orthene	organophosphate	fast	short
bendiocarb	Turcam	carbamate	intermediate	intermediate
bifenthrin	Talstar	synthetic pyrethroid	fast or intermediate	intermediate
carbaryl	Sevin, Sevimol	carbamate	intermediate	intermediate
chlorpyrifos	Dursban	organophosphate	intermediate	intermediate
cyfluthrin	Tempo	synthetic pyrethroid	fast or intermediate	intermediate
cyhalothrin	Battle, Scimitar	synthetic pyrethroid	fast or intermediate	intermediate
ethoprop	Mocap	organophosphate	fast	intermediate
fipronil	Choice	phenylpyrazole	slow	very long
fonofos	Crusade, Mainstay	organophosphate	intermediate	intermediate
imidacloprid	Merit	chloronicotinyl	very slow	long or very long
isazofos	Triumph	organophosphate	fast	long
isofenphos	Oftanol	organophosphate	slow	long
trichlorfon	Dylox, Proxol	organophosphate	fast	short

[1] Example names given; not a complete list.
[2] Speed of efficacy: fast=1 to 3 days; intermediate= 3 to 7 days; slow=7 to 14 days; very slow=more than 2 weeks. Guideline only, varies with weather conditions.
[3] Residual effect: short=1 to 2 weeks; intermediate=3 to 6 weeks; long=4 to 8 weeks; very long=more than 10 weeks. Guideline only, varies with weather conditions.

Non-target effects: Is there a population of beneficial insects which you should be careful to protect? Is the material you are considering a broad-spectrum material, i.e., will it have a detrimental effect on beneficial insects? Often there is an active population of predators in the turf, so try to avoid applying broad-spectrum materials when those predators are most active.

Biological controls: Are you using any biological control strategies (entomopathogenic nematodes, bacteria, fungi, predators, parasites)? If so, is the insecticide compatible with that strategy?

Local conditions: Identify any local environmental conditions that must be considered. Do you have ponds or streams running through the golf course or near the golf course? Is your soil sandy and subject to leaching following intense rain or irrigation? Do you have areas that are compacted, increasing the likelihood of runoff? Is the turf healthy, or do you have bare patches where insecticides might penetrate more quickly?

Speed of action: Determine whether you need a fast-acting material (Are the insects already feeding actively in the larval or nymphal stages?) or if you can use a slower-acting but long-lasting material (Are the insects just beginning to hatch?).

Application method: Do you have a preference for a granular product or a sprayable formulation?

Irrigation: Do you have the ability to irrigate after (or sometimes before) an application?

Water pH: What is your water pH? Is the insecticide sensitive to that pH?

Chemical class: Do not use materials from the same chemical class repeatedly in the same location or more than once per pest generation. Insects sometimes develop the ability to detoxify, or break down, certain kinds of chemicals to the point where the material is no longer effective. Usually insects that are resistant to one chemical in a group will be resistant to all chemicals in that group even though you have not used them in that site.

There are many insecticides available for use on turf, with a range of activities and characteristics. Take time to study the literature and determine which ones are most suited to your needs. Add this information to your pest profiles!

FURTHER READING

Baxendale, F.P. Billbugs: Characteristics and Control. *Golf Course Management.* 58(4)115–118, 1990.

Baxendale, F.P. and R.E. Cassoin, Eds. *Integrated Turfgrass Management for the Northern Great Plains.* Cooperative Extension, Institute of Agriculture and Natural Resources, University of Nebraska, Lincoln, NE, 1997.

Brandenburg, R.L. Effective Management of Subsurface Turf Pests. *Golf Course Management.* 63(12):61–64, 1995.

Brandenburg, R.L. and M.G. Villani, Eds. *Handbook of Turfgrass Insects Pests.* Entomological Society of America, Lanham, MD, 1996.

Cobb, P.P. Insect Control on the Golf Course: A Major Linkage with Irrigation. *Golf Course Irrigation.* 4(2):12–14, 1996.

Cobb, P.P. and K.R. Lewis. Searching for the Best Ways to Control Mole Crickets. *Golf Course Management.* 58(6):26–28, 32–34, 1990.

Fermanian, R.W., M.C. Shurtleff, R. Randell, H.T. Wilkinson, and P.L. Nixon. *Controlling Turfgrass Pests.* Prentice-Hall, Inc., Upper Saddle River, NJ, 1997.

Hudson, W.G. Life Cycles and Population Monitoring of Pest Mole Crickets, in *Handbook of Integrated Pest Management for Turf and Ornamentals*, Leslie, A.R., Ed., Lewis Publishers, Boca Raton, FL, 1994.

Shetlar, D.J. Managing Black Cutworms Without Pesticides. *Golf Course Management.* 63(4):49–51, 1995.

Sparks, B. and S.K. Braman. Decision-Making Factors for Management of Fire Ants and White Grubs in Turfgrass, in *Handbook of Integrated Pest Management for*

Turf and Ornamentals, Leslie, A.R., Ed., Lewis Publishers, Boca Raton, FL, 1994.

Stahnke, G. and A. Antonelli. European Crane Flies in the Pacific Northwest. *Golf Course Management*. 63(12):56–60, 1995.

Tashiro, H. *Turfgrass Insects of the United States and Canada*. Cornell University Press, Ithaca, NY, 1987.

Villani, M.G. Focus on biological controls. *TurfGrass Trends* 4(6):1–6, 1995.

Villani, M.G. Relationships among soil insects, soil insecticides, and soil physical properties. *TurfGrass Trends* 4(9):11–17, 1995.

Villani, M.G. A Year in the Life of a Japanese Beetle. *Golf Course Management*. 58(7):14–22, 1990.

Villani, M.G., S.R. Krueger, and J. Nyrop. A Case Study of the Impact of the Soil Environment on Insect/Pathogen Interactions: Scarabs in Turfgrass, in *Handbook of Integrated Pest Management for Turf and Ornamentals*, Leslie, A.R., Ed., Lewis Publishers, Boca Raton, FL, 1994.

Vittum, P.J. Effective Control of White Grubs. *Golf Course Management*. 60(7)18–20, 24–28, 1992.

Vittum, P.J. Back to Basics — Insecticide Primer. *TurfGrass Trends*. Part One: What Insecticides Can and Cannot Do. 5(8):1–8, 1996. Part Two: Chemical Classes of Turfgrass Insecticides. 6(1):9–17, 1997. Part Three: Insecticide Formulations. 6(4):1–8, 1997.

Watschke, T.L., P.H. Dernoeden, and D.J. Shetlar. *Managing Turfgrass Pests*. Lewis Publishers, Boca Raton, FL, 1995.

CHAPTER 8

PEST MANAGEMENT: DISEASES

GENERAL BIOLOGY

As with other turfgrass pests, integrated disease management is *stress* management. To develop an integrated management program, it is important to understand exactly what problems are truly diseases. Although turfgrass injuries or disorders may look like diseases, they are not diseases and should not be treated as such.

Injury

Injury is a destructive physical occurrence.

Examples: lightning strike (Figure 8.1), shoe spike damage, divots, golf cart trails, hydraulic fluid leaks, pesticide damage

No living organism caused the damage observed, so it will not spread to other areas. Some injuries are preventable, whereas others are beyond your control. Concentrate on preventing or limiting the damage that you can anticipate.

Control Example: Spiked shoes can injure turfgrass. Discuss limiting spikes on the golf course with golf pro and golfers. Suggest an alternative such as the "soft spike" golf shoes recommended by the USGA.

Disorder

Disorder is an interaction between the plant and its environment that is usually associated with imbalances (too much or too little) of certain physical or chemical requirements for turfgrass growth.

Examples: excessive rainfall, drought, nutritional deficiencies or imbalances, cold or heat stress, winter desiccation

Photo 8.1. Lightning damage on a golf green. (Courtesy P.P. Cobb.)

No living organism caused the disorder, so it will not spread to other areas. Disorders weaken turfgrass and increase their susceptibility to pests and diseases. Concentrate on preventing or limiting the damage due to disorders.

Control Example: Greens covers can help prevent winter desiccation. Care must be taken, however, to be sure that proper ventilation occurs under the cover. Accumulation of moisture is conducive to the growth of snow mold fungi.

Disease

Disease is an interaction between the plant and a pathogen that disrupts the normal growth and appearance of the plant.

Turfgrass disease development requires three components:

1. susceptible turfgrass **host** (always present)
2. virulent **pathogen** (always present)

Figure 8.2. The striped pattern suggests a noninfectious problem. (Courtesy M.L. Elliott.)

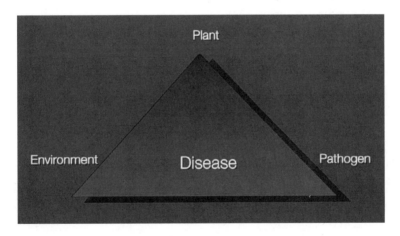

Figure 8.3. The disease triangle is a reminder that three factors are necessary for disease: the plant, the pathogen, and favorable environmental conditions. (Courtesy G.L. Schumann.)

3. conducive **environment** in which the host and pathogen interact (changes frequently)

Environment may predispose the plant to infection by the pathogen, but the environmental conditions are not the *direct* cause of the disease observed.

Any stress (environmental or of human origin) placed on turf will weaken the turf and make it more susceptible to disease development.

Concentrate on managing the environment of each individual area on the golf course to manage potential disease problems.

Control Example: One bentgrass green is in an open area with lots of air circulation. A second green is surrounded by trees, resulting in minimal air circulation. The amount of the disease causal agent, *Pythium*, is the same on both greens. For Pythium blight to occur, the maximum temperature must exceed 86°F (30°C) with more than 14 hr of relative humidity > 90%. These environmental conditions usually occur only on the second green, which is also the green where Pythium blight occurs most frequently. Installation of fans, or tree removal, will help limit Pythium blight on the second green by increasing air circulation to decrease temperature and dry the leaf tissue.

Turfgrass Pathogens

Fungi are the primary pathogens observed on turfgrass. Fungi are unable to produce their own energy and must rely on living or dead hosts for energy and growth.

Most fungi are totally harmless, using only dead organic matter for growth. These fungi are extremely important in turfgrass as decay organisms that help reduce thatch, and as competitive organisms that help provide natural biological controls.

A few specialized fungi cause turfgrass diseases under certain environmental conditions. When a fungal pathogen is not actively invading a plant, it is surviving in a state of dormancy (as a spore or sclerotium) or living on dead organic matter in the thatch or soil.

DISEASE DIAGNOSIS

Before jumping to the conclusion that a turf problem is caused by a fungus, look carefully at the symptoms on the site. Try to eliminate injuries or disorders as causes of the symptoms observed. Only you know the recent activity level, weather conditions, and fertilizer and pesticide applications that might be causing the problem. Remember that many fungi will readily invade dead or dying plant tissue even when the original cause of the problem was some type of physical injury.

Two clues that a problem is caused by a fungal pathogen:

1. **Circular** spots or patches of disease: (Figures 8.4 and 8.5)
   These are caused by the outward, radial growth of the fungal mycelia from a central point.

Figure 8.4. The small *circular* spots of dollar spot suggest a fungal disease. (Courtesy M.L. Elliott.)

Figure 8.5. The large *circular* patches of bermudagrass decline also suggest a fungal disease. (Courtesy M.L. Elliott.)

2. Weblike **mycelia** and/or masses of **spores** that appear in wet conditions: (Figures 8.6 and 8.7)
   Fungal activity is best observed early in the morning when dew is present, after irrigation, or during rainy weather. Mycelia disappear quickly once the turf dries.

Many of the pathogens that cause plant diseases have the ability to exist as both disease-causing pathogens and as saprophytes on plants or in soil. Any turfgrass sample will include a number of possible pathogens, but their pres-

Figure 8.6. In moist weather, Typhula blight (gray snow mold) can usually be separated from Fusarium patch (pink snow mold) by the color of the mycelium growing on the surface of the turfgrass. See Color Plate 20. (Courtesy G.L. Schumann.)

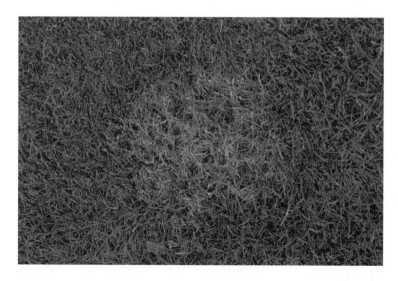

Figure 8.7. Red thread disease is diagnosed by the red mycelium and pink spores of the fungus. See Color Plate 19. (Courtesy G.L. Schumann.)

Figure 8.8. A pink snow mold sample upon arrival at a diagnostic laboratory. See Color Plate 21. (Courtesy G.L. Schumann.)

ence does not necessarily implicate them in the disease problem. The quality of the turfgrass sample will often determine whether a diagnostician can interpret the presence of pathogens in a sample as the likely cause of the disease symptoms. Diagnosticians are well-trained, but they are not able to create something out of nothing.

To Obtain a Sample for Disease Diagnosis (Figure 8.8)

1. Sample problematic turf areas *before* the application of pesticides, especially fungicides. If you cannot ship the sample the same day you take it, place it in the refrigerator until you can ship it.
2. Always sample from the marginal areas of symptomatic turfgrass, not from a totally dead area. Samples representing various stages of disease development are the best.
3. Areas of turf expressing symptoms of wilt, poor color, slow thinning, or melting-out should be diagnosed for fungal problems and nematodes. Directions for taking a soil sample for nematodes are described in Chapter 9.
4. The fungal disease sample should be *at least* a 4-inch (10 cm) diameter plug of turfgrass that has been dug, not pulled, from the turf area. Use a cup cutter and provide 2 to 3 inches (5 to 8 cm) of roots and soil below the thatch.
5. Samples should be packed and shipped such that the plant symptoms remain relatively unchanged when they arrive at a clinic. Do not add water. Do not seal tightly in plastic. Wrap the sample in several layers of newspaper and pack it snugly in a box so soil does not shake onto sample surface.

6. *Each* sample must be accompanied by a completed form appropriate for your clinic. Plants don't talk. The information required must come from you! Since a number of pathogens can cause the same symptoms, it is extremely important to know the history of the turf sample, including:

   a. symptoms: appearance, pattern relative to mowing direction, compacted areas, low areas, areas with poor air circulation, etc.
   b. turf species and cultivar, if known
   c. environmental conditions when symptoms first occurred
   d. recent pesticide and fertilizer applications
   e. other recent management practices, such as aeration, vertical cutting
   f. soil type and pH

   Keep the form separate from the sample. Place it in a separate plastic bag so it does not become soggy or illegible or tear easily when touched.

7. Color photographs are *always* useful, as they often describe the disease situation better than words.

8. Deliver directly to the diagnostic lab or use an express service that delivers to the diagnostic lab itself rather than a large institutional mail room. In some areas, you may want to call ahead to discuss the problem with the diagnostician for advice in taking an appropriate sample.

Develop a pest profile for each disease! (See Chapter 2)

ENVIRONMENTAL FACTORS THAT AFFECT DISEASE DEVELOPMENT

Once you know that a turfgrass problem is a disease, it is important to understand the factors that influence disease development. Environmental factors are the most common influences on disease occurrence. Sudden or prolonged weather changes cannot be controlled, but the microenvironment of individual areas of a golf course can be modified through cultural practices and landscape modifications.

Important environmental factors to monitor include:

- Leaf wetness
- Relative humidity
- Wind speed and direction
- Day length
- Solar radiation

- Air and soil temperatures
- Soil moisture and drainage
- Soil pH
- Soil fertility

These environmental factors can affect the pathogens directly. Fungi require water for spore germination, mycelial growth, and infection of the plant leaves and roots. Water also disperses fungi across the turf and in the soil. These same environmental factors also affect the plants. When plants are stressed, they are more vulnerable to infection by pathogens.

> To me, making a commitment to integrated pest management means getting back to good sound turf management practices. In the private club sector where budgets run high, it becomes very easy to get away from the so-called "basics" of turf management. Why take the chance when I can spray for every pest under the sun every 5 to 7 days? This kind of thinking is what has gotten us into trouble with chemical resistance. But getting back to timely aeration, proper watering practices and keeping the plant in proper nutritional balance gives the turf plant a fighting chance against weeds, insects, and disease. This, in turn, allows the turf manager to feel comfortable about the health of his turf, while monitoring for the signs and thresholds that will dictate a response with chemicals.
>
> — Paul J. Jamrog, Golf Course Superintendent, Metacomet Country Club, East Providence, Rhode Island

CULTURAL CONTROL STRATEGIES

Cultural practices should promote an environment that is *not* conducive to pathogen infection and disease development. If a disease should affect the turfgrass, these practices should be implemented first or, at the very least, implemented at the same time that fungicides are applied. If a particular putting green, tee, or fairway has a history of developing a particular disease at a particular time of year, then it makes sense to implement cultural practices early to minimize this yearly recurrence.

Habits are hard to break. If changing a practice will prevent problems later, then maybe it is reasonable to change that practice. Explain to the golfers or course owner your reasons for altering a practice. Provide them with records indicating disease outbreaks, factors associated with disease outbreaks, cost of fungicide applications, etc. Explain the potential benefits of altering a maintenance practice in both economical and ecological terms.

Turfgrass Selection Strategies

The best method for controlling diseases is to prevent their occurrence. Turfgrasses that are not suited for a particular area or use will be continually stressed, more susceptible to diseases, and require increased maintenance costs in terms of labor and pesticides. If it is not practical to replace a poorly adapted turfgrass, then other cultural practices must be initiated to prevent disease occurrence.

Select turfgrass species and cultivars based on:

- Geographical location, climate, and soil
- How the turfgrass will be used *and* maintained
- Resistance to specific diseases

Limitations **to use of disease-resistant or disease-tolerant turfgrass cultivars:**

- Disease resistance is *specific*. Even though a turfgrass cultivar has resistance or tolerance to one disease, it may be highly susceptible to a different disease.
- Disease resistance may not be *permanent*. Some pathogens exist as different genetic races for which specific genes for resistance can be found in turfgrass breeding lines. These cultivars may appear to be immune to the disease when they first become available, but pathogens are capable of evolving new races that can overcome specific resistance genes. After years of use, the pathogen may overcome the resistance genes, and the turfgrass will again become diseased. In addition, different pathogen races are sometimes found in different geographical areas. Local recommendations are important for these cases. This type of resistance is not common for most turfgrass diseases. The most important example is the use of cultivar blends with resistance to various races of the leaf smut fungi.
- Some turfgrass cultivars have disease *tolerance*. These cultivars can still be infected by the pathogen, but the amount of disease that develops will be less than that of a standard cultivar under the same environmental conditions. This means that *good cultural practices can enhance disease tolerance*. It also means that poor cultural practices can cause a disease-tolerant cultivar to perform poorly and become severely diseased.

Control Examples: Bluegrasses and fine leaf fescues are very susceptible to summer patch. Creeping bentgrass, perennial ryegrass, and tall fescue are less susceptible. Likewise, bentgrasses are highly susceptible to take-all patch, but Penneagle, Providence, Regent, Carmen, Pro/Cup and Putter bentgrass cultivars have exhibited some resistance.

Mowing Strategies

Mowing is the most common turf maintenance operation. Plants produce their energy by a process called photosynthesis. A low height of cut reduces photosynthesis. In addition, diseases eventually reduce the leaf canopy, and photosynthesis is decreased even more. Raising the height of cut increases the green plant tissue needed for photosynthesis, resulting in more energy for turfgrass growth and development and, subsequently, recovery from disease.

- Turfgrasses that are cut *below* their optimum height will be stressed and more susceptible to diseases. Raise the height of cut as a preventive and curative disease control measure (Figure 8.9).
- To maintain speed on greens after raising mowing height: double cut, use rollers, topdress, and use groomer or brush attachments.
- Communicate to the golf pro, owner, and/or golfers the reasons for raising the height of cut. Try to base the information on cost of using fungicides and/or cost of *not* raising the height ("Greens will look worse if we don't raise the height").
- Turf with active leaf disease areas should be mowed last, as mowers may spread the pathogen from one location to another, resulting in a disease spreading from hole to hole in the order that golf holes were cut.

Control Example: The best curative and preventive method for controlling bermudagrass decline is to raise the height of grass. Systemic DMI fungicides are ineffective and may prolong the recovery period.

Irrigation Strategies

While irrigation is essential to prevent drought damage, the amount of water and the timing of its application can prevent or contribute to disease development. Most fungal pathogens that cause leaf diseases require a lengthy period (>10 continuous hours) of free water or very high humidity (>90%) to initiate the infection process.

- Rainfall and dew are critical factors for disease development, and are, of course, unavoidable. Irrigation, however, can be controlled by the turfgrass manager.

Figure 8.9. Bermudagrass decline occurs most often on the outside edge of a putting green in the cleanup pass due to stress from the extra mowing. (Courtesy M.L. Elliott.)

Figure 8.10. Removing dew by mowing will reduce disease activity. (Courtesy G.L. Schumann.)

- Irrigate when dew is already present (pre-dawn hours) to avoid lengthening the dew period. Since putting greens are most susceptible to diseases, irrigate greens last so they are irrigated during the pre-dawn hours.
- If localized dry spots have developed, hand watering may be required on these areas in addition to the normal irrigation cycle. During heat stress periods, it may be necessary to syringe greens. This is acceptable, as you are trying to avoid stress. Also, the leaves will dry very quickly, usually in less than 2 hours.

Figure 8.11. Proper tree pruning improves air movement and light for healthy turfgrass. (Courtesy F.D. Dinelli.)

Plant Nutrition Strategies

Many diseases are influenced by the nutritional status of the grass, especially nitrogen. A perfect balance is the goal, because both excessively high and low nitrogen fertility contribute to turfgrass diseases (Figures 8.12 and 8.13).

- Diseases that are more severe if nitrogen fertility is **low**:
  - anthracnose
  - dollar spot
  - red thread/pink patch
  - rust
- Diseases that are more severe if nitrogen fertility is **excessive**:
  - brown patch
  - Helminthosporium-type leaf spots
  - Pythium blight
  - snow molds
  - stripe smut

It is easy to quickly add **nitrogen** to the soil but impossible to remove it quickly. Use of slow-release synthetic or organic nitrogen prevents a sudden flush of leaf growth that is favorable for leaf disease development.

Potassium may help to prevent diseases, as it is linked with plant stress prevention. A non-stressed plant is not as susceptible to diseases. Potassium leaches as readily as nitrogen, so slow-release sources are advisable, especially when a slow-release nitrogen source is used, to maintain the proper nitrogen/ potassium balance.

Figure 8.12. Red thread develops when nitrogen levels are low and turf is stressed. (Courtesy G.L. Schumann.)

Figure 8.13. Dollar spot is more prevalent where nitrogen fertilizer application was missed. (Courtesy M.L. Elliott.)

All plant nutrients must be *available* to the plant — not just present in the soil. A **soil analysis** simply informs you of the nutrients present in the soil. **Leaf tissue analysis** informs you of the nutrient status of the plant.

Plate 1. Annual bluegrass weevil damage. (Courtesy P.J. Vittum.)

Plate 2. Annual bluegrass weevil larva. (Courtesy New York State Turfgrass Association.)

Plate 3. Brown patch with active mycelia in early morning hours when dew is still present. (Courtesy G.L. Schumann.)

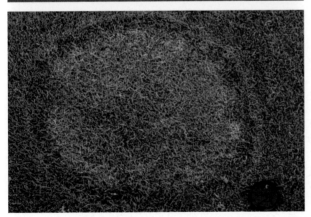

Plate 4. Symptoms of brown patch on colonial bentgrass. (Courtesy G.L. Schumann.)

Plate 5. Characteristic mycelia and spores of the fungus that causes red thread makes diagnosis quite easy in humid weather. (Courtesy G.L. Schumann.)

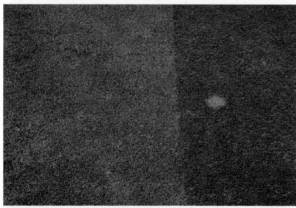

Plate 6. In humid weather, the heavy white mycelium of the fungus that causes dollar spot may be easily mistaken for *Pythium.* (Courtesy G.L. Schumann.)

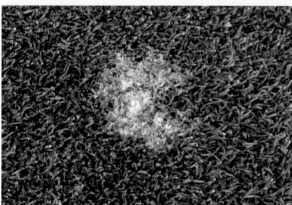

Plate 7. Low mowing height enhances bermudagrass decline in summer (close-up): left 3/16"; right 1/4". (Courtesy M.L. Elliott.)

Plate 8. Pythium blight spread by water. (Courtesy M.L. Elliott.)

Plate 9. Cultivar evaluation trial of bermudagrass maintained as putting greens mowed at 1/8". (Courtesy M.L. Elliott.)

Plate 10. Brown patch (*Rhizoctonia solani*) resistance in creeping bentgrass (healthy plots) compared to colonial bentgrass plot (diseased plot). (Courtesy G.L. Schumann.)

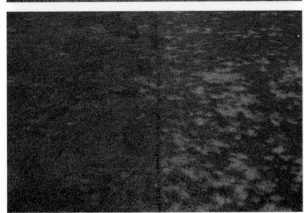

Plate 11. These naturally infected plots vary only in the amount of nitrogen fertilizer they have received. The low-nitrogen plot on the right has dollar spot; the high-nitrogen plot on the left has brown patch. (Courtesy G.L. Schumann.)

Plate 12. Thatch layer in turf that has not been cultivated in more than one year. (Courtesy M.L. Elliott.)

Plate 13. Optimal uniform organic layer in soil when aeration is performed regularly. (Courtesy M.L. Elliott.)

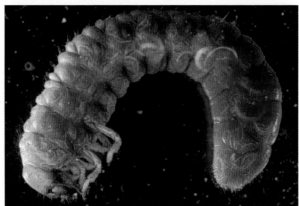

Plate 14. Third instar June beetle grub (*Phyllophaga* sp.) parasitized by tachinid fly larvae. (Courtesy M.G. Villani.)

Plate 15. Third instar Japanese beetle grub infected by the nematode *Heterorhabditis bacteriophora*. Both infective immatures (dauers) and adult nematodes are visible. (Courtesy M.G. Villani.)

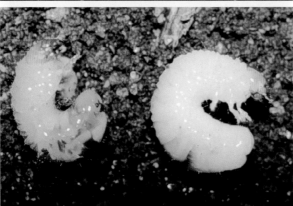

Plate 16. Third instar black turfgrass ataenius grub with milky disease caused by a *Bacillus* bacterium (right), compared to a healthy grub (left). (Courtesy M.G. Villani.)

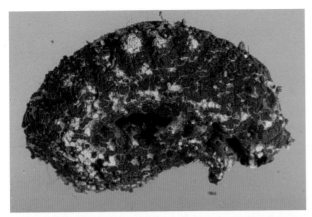

Plate 17. Third instar Japanese beetle grub infected by the fungus *Metarhizium anisopliae.* (Courtesy M.G. Villani.)

Plate 18. Third instar Japanese beetle grub that failed to molt properly when treated with an insect growth regulator (IGR). (Courtesy M.G. Villani.)

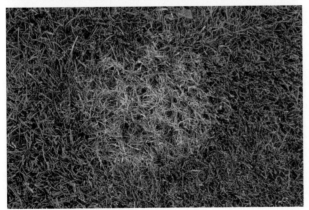

Plate 19. Red thread disease is diagnosed by the red mycelium and pink spores of the fungus. (Courtesy G.L. Schumann.)

Plate 20. In moist weather, Typhula blight (gray snow mold) can usually be separated from Fusarium patch (pink snow mold) by the color of the mycelium growing on the surface of the turfgrass. (Courtesy G.L. Schumann.)

Plate 21. A pink snow mold sample upon arrival at a diagnostic laboratory. (Courtesy G.L. Schumann.)

Plate 22. Excess thatch. (Courtesy J. Bresnahan.)

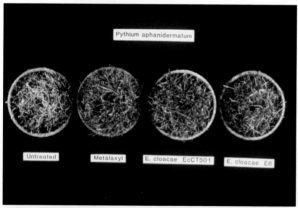

Plate 23. Use of an introduced bacterium, *Enterobacter cloacae,* for biocontrol of Pythium blight. (Courtesy E.B. Nelson.)

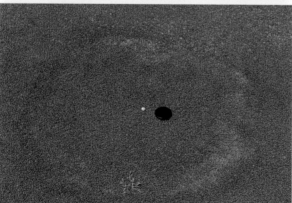

Plate 24. Necrotic fairy rings due to *Lycoperdon* (puffball mushroom). (Courtesy M.L. Elliott.)

Plate 25. Necrotic rings due to *Rhizoctonia zeae.* Even though the symptoms are similar, fungicide choices may be different. Accurate diagnosis is essential. (Courtesy M.L. Elliott.)

Plate 26. *Hoplolaimus* nematodes in a turfgrass root. They are stained red and several can be seen lengthwise in the cortical root tissue. (Courtesy R.L. Wick.)

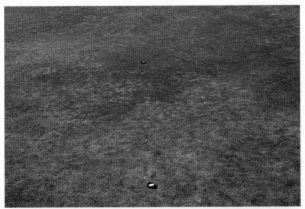

Plate 27. Symptoms of lance and stunt nematode injury to annual bluegrass on a putting green in New England. (Courtesy R.L. Wick.)

Plate 28. View of sting nematode damage of "Tifdwarf" bermudagrass. (Courtesy M.L. Elliott.)

Plate 29. Close-up of same site (as Plate 27) showing weed infestation of the weakened turfgrass. (Courtesy M.L. Elliott.)

Plate 30. Perennial weed (yellow nutsedge) with rhizomes and tubers. (Courtesy J.C. Neal.)

Plate 31. Compacted soil core on the left is from the weedy area with poorly growing turfgrass and a large infestation of broadleaf plantain. Soil core on the right is from a much less compacted area nearby with fewer weeds and better turf quality. (Courtesy J.C. Neal.)

Plate 32. A greenhouse biocontrol experiment using the fungus *Sclerotinia sclerotiorum* against plantain. (Courtesy J.C. Neal.)

Plant utilization of nutrients is a *dynamic* process, so your fertilization practices should be also. Modifications will be required as the season progresses and from year to year.

Thatch Control Strategies

Thatch is the tightly bound layer of living and dead stems and roots that develops between the zone of green vegetation and the soil surface. It is a natural and desirable component of a turfgrass ecosystem. An *excessive* thatch (Figure 8.15) accumulation indicates that an imbalance has occurred and plant tissue is being produced more quickly than it is being decomposed.

- Fungi (turfgrass pathogens included), bacteria, nematodes, and insects all help decompose thatch.
- Factors that **impede microbial decomposition:**
  - excessively wet or dry conditions
  - very high or low thatch pH
  - inadequate nitrogen levels
  - repeated use of chemical pesticides
- Excess thatch increases the population of fungi that can *potentially* cause a disease if the proper environmental conditions develop. Therefore, a goal in preventing excessive thatch is to **reduce disease potential.**
- Excess thatch may also create a stressful environment, especially when the thatch layer becomes hydrophobic (repels water). Roots may live in the thatch and never move into the soil layer.

BIOLOGICAL CONTROL STRATEGIES

Biological control of diseases means that another living organism is actively involved in suppressing or preventing the growth of the pathogen, either in the soil/thatch region or on/in the plant. This can be accomplished by microorganisms naturally present in the turfgrass ecosystem, by introducing specific microorganisms, or by applying organic materials that alter the natural microorganism populations. Microorganisms suppress diseases using many methods. Three common methods include:

- Biologicals **exclude** the pathogen from the plant simply by occupying the space first.
- Biologicals can **outcompete** the pathogen for food sources. In other words, they starve the pathogen, so it cannot grow and infect the plant.
- Biologicals can produce **toxins** (natural poisons) that suppress the growth of the fungus. The biologicals act as little chemical factories,

Figure 8.14. When the soil pH was lowered too quickly with elemental sulfur, St. Augustinegrass was killed. Avoid drastic changes in the soil environment. (Courtesy M.L. Elliott.)

Figure 8.15. Excess thatch. See Color Plate 22. (Courtesy J. Bresnahan.)

but the chemicals produced are usually very specific in nature. Environmental exposure is minimal because very small amounts are being produced in a very limited area.

Natural Biological Control

Microorganisms naturally present in the turfgrass ecosystem need to be managed just as carefully as the turf is managed. This requires careful use of *all* chemi-

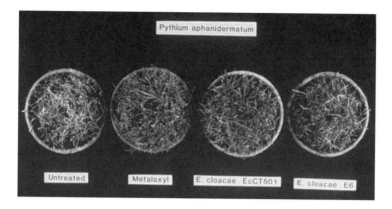

Figure 8.16. Use of an introduced bacterium, *Enterobacter cloacae*, for biocontrol of Pythium blight. See Color Plate 23. (Courtesy E.B. Nelson.)

cal pesticides. Pesticides can reduce beneficial organisms as well as pests. (See Chapter 5.)

Introduction of Specific Organisms

Just as there are no "miracle" fungicides for disease control, there will be no "miracle" or "silver bullet" biological control agents or composts. Biological controls are just one more strategy to consider in a well-planned IPM program.

The first commercial biological control agents for turfgrass have recently been registered with the EPA. One is a fungus, *Trichoderma harzianum* (Biotrek) which is available in a granular formulation. Another is a bacterium, *Pseudomonas aureofaceans* (BioJect), which is applied through the irrigation system. There are few reports from scientifically designed experiments about what diseases are best controlled by these products, or about their consistency as disease control agents. However, it should be remembered that fungicides do not always work very well either. The following research examples demonstrate the potential of biocontrol for turfgrass diseases (Tables 8.1 and 8.2). In nature, maintenance of high populations of an applied organism is unlikely. *Repeated applications* will probably be necessary, as with fungicides.

Current **limitations** of the use of specific biocontrol organisms for turf diseases include:

- Proper timing of applications.
  They will only be effective for preventive disease control.
- Large-scale commercial production of the organisms.
- Formulation challenges to maintain viability and shelf-life of the product.

Table 8.1. Antagonistic organisms applied in water as a spray or as a topdressing with an organic carrier such as cornmeal.

Specific Organism	General Group	Diseases Controlled
Enterobacter cloacae	Bacterium	dollar spot Pythium blight Pythium root rot
Pseudomonas spp.	Bacterium	Pythium blight take-all patch
Gliocladium virens	Fungus	brown patch dollar spot
Fusarium heterosporum	Fungus	dollar spot
Trichoderma spp.	Fungus	dollar spot Pythium blight southern blight Typhula blight

Table 8.2. Fungi that are closely related to pathogens, but do not cause disease themselves.

Specific Organism	General Group	Diseases Controlled
Binucleate *Rhizoctonia* spp.	Fungus	brown patch
Typhula phacorrhiza	Fungus	Typhula blight
Gaeumannomyces spp.	Fungus	take-all patch

Disease-Suppressive Composts and Other Organic Materials

Certain composts have been shown to suppress the following turfgrass diseases:

- Brown patch
- Dollar spot (Figure 8.17)
- Necrotic ring spot
- Pythium blight
- Pythium root rot
- Red thread
- Typhula blight (gray snow mold)

Current **limitations** to the use of composts and natural organic fertilizers for turf diseases include:

- Not all composts are disease-suppressive. In fact, the actual microbial inoculation of most composted materials is mostly accidental and depends on what organisms are present at the time the process is completed. As researchers determine which organisms give a compost its suppressiveness, some companies are deliberately adding certain organisms to their composts to help ensure disease suppres-

Figure 8.17. Use of compost for biocontrol of dollar spot. Non-treated (foreground plot), propiconazole fungicide (center plot), and compost (back plot). (Courtesy E.B. Nelson.)

sion. However, the details of this science are not completely understood, and reliable quality control of composts for disease suppression still lies in the future.

- A second broad generalization is that although some composts appear to be fairly consistent in their ability to suppress certain diseases, composts do not generally suppress all turf diseases. Before purchasing a compost for its disease suppressiveness, check on recent field research in your area for the latest results.

CHEMICAL CONTROL STRATEGIES

Chemical control of fungal turfgrass diseases is accomplished by using fungicides. It is acceptable to use fungicides on a preventive basis as long as you truly understand what diseases/pathogens you are protecting the grass from at any given time of the year. Why apply a fungicide for a particular disease if that disease has never been observed on your course or is very rare for the grass you are growing? Remember that the primary factor for turfgrass disease development is the environment — not just the overall environment, but the *microenvironment* created by the landscape situation and your management practices.

- Fungicides do not *eliminate* the pathogens from the turfgrass area, but primarily *suppress* the growth of the fungal pathogens to prevent them from infecting the plant during the time period when the environment is conducive to disease development.
- Overuse of fungicides has the potential to increase or shift the disease spectrum on turfgrasses, lead to development of fungicide-resistant strains of pathogens, and increase thatch development.
- You would not think of giving a family member any medication without reading the instructions first, so treat your grass the same way.
  - How much water should you use?
  - Do you need an adjuvant?
    Most labels specify *not* to use an adjuvant, especially surfactants. Why? Most fungicides already have a surfactant as part of their formulation.
  - What chemicals are safe for tank-mixing?
- It is to your advantage to be a good consumer, so you do not waste fungicides. Excessive or incorrect use of fungicides is expensive, and potentially harmful to the turfgrass ecosystem.
- Diseases and factors for disease development can vary from region to region. Fungicide use should vary accordingly. Rely on *local* research and *local* recommendations for fungicide use. Just because a product is effective on bentgrass in North Carolina does not mean it will be effective on bermudagrass in California.

Types of Fungicides (Table 8.3)

Contact Fungicides

- Remain on the plant surface and do *not* penetrate into the plant. They *prevent* pathogens from penetrating the plant. They do not affect pathogens that have already penetrated the plant.
- Are generally applied to the *leaf and stem surfaces*. Must be *uniformly* applied to the plant surface for effective disease control.
- Remain active only as long as the fungicide remains on the plant in sufficient concentration to inhibit fungi. Usually effective 7 to 14 days. Leaves that emerge after the fungicide has been applied will *not* be protected.
- Mow *prior* to a contact fungicide application. Otherwise, you are removing the fungicide just applied.
- Fungicide on the plant surface gradually will be lost due to:
  - mowing
  - irrigation or rainfall
  - degradation

- They are often mixed with localized-penetrant or systemic fungicides to obtain a fungicide mixture with broad-spectrum control or to enhance the activity of the penetrant fungicide.

Localized-Penetrant Fungicides

- Penetrate the plant surface but only move into the underlying tissue. They do not move within the xylem or phloem tissue. The majority of fungicide applied remains on or near the plant surface.
- Act primarily to prevent fungal infection of the plant. Usually effective for 14 to 21 days.
- Information on contact fungicides is applicable to this group.

Systemic Fungicides

- Penetrate the plant and are then translocated (move) within the plant, either in the xylem (upward) or phloem (primarily downward but some upward also) tissue. They work inside the plant to suppress fungal growth. They have curative and protective effects, with extended residual activity.
- Fosetyl-Al is the only systemic fungicide that moves significantly both upward and downward. All other fungicides in this group move primarily upward (**acropetal systemics**).
- Once inside the plant, penetrant systemic fungicides will not be removed by rain or irrigation. Newly emerged leaves may contain sufficient concentrations of the fungicide to protect them from fungal infection. Therefore, systemic fungicides do not need to be applied as often as contact fungicides; usually 14- to 28-day intervals are adequate.
- May be used for root diseases if applied in high volumes of water or drenched in immediately after application.

Fungicide Chemical Classes

Fungicides are also divided into classes based on their chemical properties (Table 8.3). To prevent fungicide resistance from developing in a pathogen population, it is important to know which fungicides belong to the same chemical class or have the same mode of action.

- Alternate or mix fungicides belonging to *different chemical classes* to prevent fungicide resistance.
- *Trade names are not an indication of the chemical class.* Alternating between trade names is *not* necessarily alternating between chemical classes.

Table 8.3. Turfgrass fungicides classified by chemical class.

Chemical Class	Common Name	Trade Name Example	Chemical Name
Acylalanine (Acropetal Systemic: xylem)	metalaxyl	Subdue	N-(2,6-dimethylphenyl)-N-(methoxyacetyl) alanine methyl ester
Aromatic Hydrocarbons (Contact)	chloroneb	Terraneb	1,4-dichloro-2,5-dimethoxybenzene
	ethazol/ etridiazole	Koban	5-ethoxy-3-trichloromethyl-1,2,4-thiadiazole
	PCNB/ quintozene	Terraclor	pentachloronitrobenzene
Benzamide (Acropetal Systemic: xylem)	flutolanil	ProStar	N-[3-(1-methylethoxy)phenyl]-2-(trifluoromethyl)benzamide
Benzimidazole (Acropetal Systemic: xylem)	thiophanate-methyl	Fungo	dimethyl 4,4'-o-phenylenebis[3-thioallophanate]
Benzonitrile (Contact)	chlorothalonil	Daconil 2787	tetrachloroisophthalonitrile
Carbamate (Acropetal Systemic: xylem)	propamocarb	Banol	propyl[3-(dimethylamino)propyl]carbamate monohydrochloride

Class	Common name	Trade name	Chemical name
Dicarboximides (Localized Penetrant)	iprodione	Chipco 26019	3-(3,5-dichlorophenyl)-N-(1-methylethyl)-2,4-dioxo-1-imidazolidinecarboxamide
	vinclozolin	Curalan	3-(3,5-dichlorophenyl)-5-ethenyl-5-methyl-2,4-oxazolidinedione
Demethylation Inhibitors (DMIs, Triazoles, Sterol Inhibitors) (Acropetal Systemic: xylem)	cyproconazole	Sentinel	α-(4-chlorophenyl)-a-(1-cyclopropylethyl)-1H-1,2,4-triazole-1-ethanol
	fenarimol	Rubigan	α-(2-chlorophenyl)-a-(4-chlorophenyl)-5-pyrimidinemethanol
	myclobutanil	Eagle	α-butyl-a-(chlorophenyl)-1H-1,2,4-triazole-1-propanenitrile
	propiconazole	Banner	1-{[2-(2,4-dichlorophenyl)4-propyl-1,3-dioxolan-2-yl]methyl}-1H-1,2,4-triazole
	triadimefon	Bayleton	1-(4-cmhlorophenoxy)-3,3-dimethyl-1-(1H-1,2,4-triazol-1-yl)-2-butanone
Dithiocarbamates (Contact)	mancozeb	Dithane DF	coordination product of zinc ion and manganese ethylene bisdithiocarbamate
	maneb	Manex	manganese ethylene bisdithiocarbamate
	thiram	Spotrete	tetramethylthiuram disulfide
Ethyl Phosphonate (Systemic: phloem)	fosetyl-Al	Aliette	aluminum tris (O-ethyl phosphonate)
B-Methoxyacrylate (Acropetal Systemic: xylem)	azoxystrobin	Heritage	methyl(E)-2-{2-[6-(2-cyanophenoxy)pyrimidin-4-yloxy]phenyl}-3-methoxy-acrylate

- Marketing of fungicide mixtures makes it very important to know the chemical names or common names of fungicides. Fungicides that contain mixtures of active ingredients will not list on the label the individual trade names of the ingredients in the mixture.
- If you do not achieve disease control with a fungicide, make sure the disease was properly diagnosed and the fungicide properly applied before assuming that a fungicide-resistant strain has developed.
- Do not mix or sequentially use DMI fungicides (triazoles) with triazole-type plant growth regulators such as paclobutrazol and flurprimidol.

Selecting a Fungicide

- **Efficacy on target pathogen/disease:** Is the pathogen attacking the leaves or the roots? The answer to that question should determine your fungicide selection and how you will apply the material. Determine what the local recommendations are, and read the fungicide label completely (Figures 8.18 and 8.19).
- **Safety to the turfgrass:** Is the fungicide labelled for the target turfgrass in that particular site at that particular time of year?
- **Non-target effects:** Overuse of fungicides can result in reduced populations of natural biological control organisms. This may enhance disease development.
- **Application method:** Granules vs. sprays; sprays vs. drench. When applying contact or local-penetrant fungicides as a spray, and the target is a leaf pathogen, the fungicide must be applied in a *minimum* of 2 gallons of water per 1000 square feet (815 L/ha) in order to obtain thorough coverage of the leaf surface. Drenching or post-application irrigation may be required if the pathogen target is on the roots, or when trying to control fairy rings.
- **Application timing:** Fungicides should be applied prior to predicted disease development or soon after disease symptoms are first observed.
- **Irrigation:** If necessary, can you irrigate after an application? If not, fungicides should be applied in a high volume of water.
- **Adjuvants:** Read the label carefully to determine if one is needed, especially surfactants or wetting agents, as most fungicides are already formulated with an adjuvant. However, it may be necessary to add a buffering agent if your water pH is too high or too low.
- **Longevity:** If a second application is necessary, what is the time interval between applications listed on the label?
- **Mode and site of action:** Is the fungicide a contact, localized penetrant, or systemic? In other words, where does it work? How does it affect the pathogen?

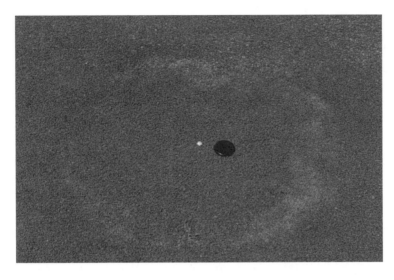

Figure 8.18. Necrotic fairy rings due to *Lycoperdon* sp. (puffball mushroom). See Color Plate 24. (Courtesy M.L. Elliott.)

Figure 8.19. Necrotic rings due to *Rhizoctonia zeae*. Even though the symptoms are similar, fungicide choices may be different. Accurate diagnosis is essential. See Color Plate 25. (Courtesy M.L. Elliott.)

- **Chemical class:** Have you used this chemical class before? It is critical not to use the same chemical class repeatedly to avoid development of resistance in the target fungus.

Resistance Management

As with all pesticides, repeated use of fungicides with the same mode of action may result in pathogenic fungi that are tolerant or resistant to chemicals in that group. Resistance can develop quickly in fungi because they multiply very quickly. Seek help from your local experts about how to best prevent fungicide resistance from developing on your golf course.

FURTHER READING

Baxendale, F.B. and R.E. Gaussoin, Eds. *Integrated Turfgrass Management for the Northern Great Plains,* Cooperative Extension, Institute of Agriculture and Natural Resources, University of Nebraska, Lincoln, NE, 1997.

Burpee, L.L. *A Guide to Integrated Control of Turfgrass Diseases.* Vol. I: Cool-season turfgrasses. Vol. 2: Warm-season turfgrasses. GCSAA Publishing, Lawrence, KS, 1993 and 1995.

Clarke, B.B. and A.B. Gould, Eds. *Turfgrass Patch Diseases Caused by Ectotrophic Root-infecting Fungi,* APS Press, St. Paul, MN, 1993.

Couch, H.B. *Diseases of Turfgrasses.* Krieger Publishing Co., Malabar, FL, 1995.

Dernoeden, P.H. Collecting and Shipping Diseased Turfgrass Samples. *Golf Course Management.* 61(11):56–58, 1993.

Fermanian, T.W., M.C. Shurtleff, R. Randell, H.T. Wilkinson, and P.L. Nixon. *Controlling Turfgrass Pests,* Prentice-Hall, Inc., Upper Saddle River, NJ, 1997.

Gilhuly, L.W. Search Your Sole — Remove Your Spikes! *USGA Green Section Record.* 30(2):24, 1992.

Hagan, A. Irrigation and its Impact on Turfgrass Diseases. *Golf Course Irrigation.* 4(5):12–14, 1996.

Morrow, J. and K. Danneberger. A Look at Ball Roll. *Golf Course Management.* 63(5):54–55, 1995.

Nelson, E. *Biological Control of Turfgrass Diseases.* Cornell University, Ithaca, NY, 1992.

Nelson, E.B. Maximizing disease control with fungicide applications: The Basics of Turfgrass Fungicides. *TurfGrass Trends:* Part One: Fungicide Use and General Properties. 5(2):10–17, 1996. Part Two: Behavior in Soil. 5(3):5–11, 1996. Part Three: Plant and Pathogen Factors Affecting Fungicide Efficacy. 5(4):1–7, 1996. Part Four: Handling and Applying Fungicides. 5(8):10–15, 1996. Part Five: Record Keeping. 5(12):1–5, 1996. Part Six: Human Health and Environmental Quality Considerations. 5(12):15–18, 1996.

Nelson, E.B., L.L. Burpee, and M.B. Lawton. Biological Control of Turfgrass Diseases. In *Handbook of Integrated Pest Management for Turf and Ornamentals,* Leslie, A.R., Ed., Lewis Publishers, Boca Raton, FL, 1994.

Sanders, P. *The Microscope in Turfgrass Disease Diagnosis.* Patricia Sanders, University Park, PA, 1993.

Schumann, G.L. and J.D. MacDonald. *Turfgrass Diseases: Diagnosis and Management CD-ROM,* APS Press, St. Paul, MN, 1997.

Smiley, R.W., P.H. Dernoeden, and B.B. Clarke. *Compendium of Turfgrass Diseases,* APS Press, St. Paul, MN, 1992.

Smith, J.D., N. Jackson, and A.R. Woolhouse. *Fungal Diseases of Amenity Turf Grasses.* E.&F.N. Spon Publishers, London, 1989.

Tani, T. and J.B Beard. *Color Atlas of Turfgrass Diseases,* Ann Arbor Press, Chelsea, MI 1997.

Vargas, J. *Management of Turfgrass Diseases.* Lewis Publishers, Boca Raton, FL, 1994.

Watschke, T.L., P.H. Dernoeden, and D. Shetlar. *Managing Turfgrass Pests,* Lewis Publishers, Boca Raton, FL 1995.

Williams, D.W. and A.J. Powell, Jr. Dew Removal and Dollar Spot on Creeping Bentgrass. *Golf Course Management.* 63(8):49–52, 1995.

Further information about ongoing biocontrol research for turfgrass diseases is published annually by APS Press in *Biological and Cultural Tests for Control of Plant Diseases.*

CHAPTER **9**

PEST MANAGEMENT: NEMATODES

As with other turfgrass pests, integrated nematode management is *stress* management. In general, nematodes are actively feeding on roots when the grass is growing actively. The effects of the nematode activity often are not observed until the turfgrass is stressed, either by the weather or by human-induced environmental changes, such as compaction, mowing height, and fertility.

GENERAL BIOLOGY

Nematodes are microscopic, unsegmented round worms (Figure 9.1). Nematodes have a simple life cycle, beginning as an egg. Like many insects, they molt their cuticle (outer skin) as they develop through four juvenile stages before becoming reproducing adults.

Nematodes are found everywhere. Like fungi, most are harmless and are an important part of the natural world. However, a few nematodes are specialized parasites of turfgrass plants, spending part of their life cycle feeding on living plant material, such as turfgrass roots, in order to survive.

All plant parasitic nematodes feed with a hollow or grooved spear-like structure called a stylet. The stylet punctures the plant cell wall, injects digestive enzymes into the cell, and then withdraws the partially digested food. Plant pathogenic nematodes are divided into two groups based on feeding habit.

Ectoparasitic nematodes live on the outside of the plant surface and feed from the outside plant surface (Figure 9.1). This group is least damaging to turfgrasses, with the important exception of the sting nematode.

Endoparasitic nematodes spend at least part of their life cycle inside the roots on which they feed. They feed primarily on the inside of the roots (Figure 9.2). If they feed in one area of the root permanently, they are called "sedentary"; if they move around and feed in different areas of the root, they are called "migratory."

DIAGNOSIS OF NEMATODES AS PESTS

Symptoms alone, especially aboveground visual symptoms, are not a reliable method of diagnosing nematodes, as many diseases or disorders may result in similar damage. Diagnosis is based on symptoms observed aboveground

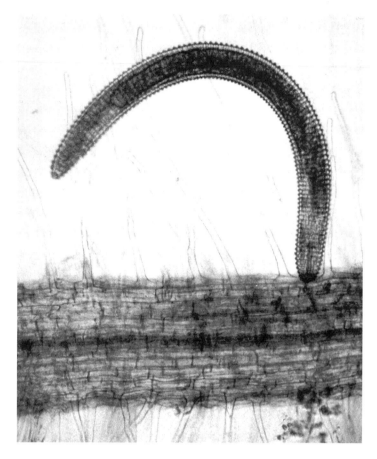

Figure 9.1. *Criconemella* nematode feeding on plant root. Note the spear-like stylet. (Courtesy S.W. Westcott III.)

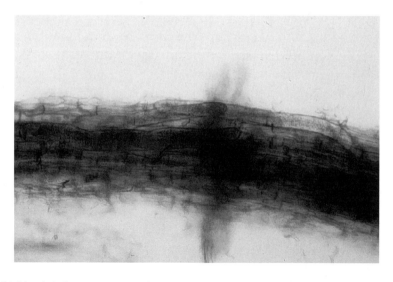

Figure 9.2. *Hoplolaimus* nematodes in a turfgrass root. They are stained red and several can be seen lengthwise in the cortical root tissue. See Color Plate 26. (Courtesy R.L. Wick.)

Figure 9.3. Symptoms of lance and stunt nematode injury to annual bluegrass on a putting green in New England. See Color Plate 27. (Courtesy R.L. Wick.)

(especially damage patterns), root symptoms, previous history, and nematode assay results (Figures 9.3 through 9.5).

Aboveground Symptoms

- Plants may be yellow, stunted, or exhibit nutrient deficiency symptoms.
- Plants wilt easily, appear drought stressed, and/or do not recover quickly after a rain or irrigation event.
- Damaged areas are most noticeable when the grass is stressed by drought, heat, etc.
- Damaged areas will become weak, resulting in weed invasions.
- Damaged areas are irregular in size and shape; they have no distinct lines.

Root Symptoms

- Roots are often very short. They may appear completely dark in color or have isolated brown or red lesions.
- Few feeder roots or root hairs are present. There may be excessive branching.
- Root tips may be discolored or appear swollen.
- Roots may be swollen or have galls.

Figure 9.4. View of sting nematode damage of "Tifdwarf" bermudagrass. See Color Plate 28. (Courtesy M.L. Elliott.)

Figure 9.5. Close-up of same site showing weed infestation of the weakened turfgrass. See Color Plate 29. (Courtesy M.L. Elliott.)

Soil Samples for Nematodes

Turfgrass can tolerate higher numbers of certain kinds of parasitic nematode species than it can of others. The only way to determine the number and type of parasitic nematodes present in an affected area is to obtain a nematode assay from the soil (Figure 9.6). Many universities and some private companies offer this service. (See additional information in Chapter 3.)

Since nematode damage can appear very similar to certain disease symptoms, it will probably be beneficial to submit a sample for disease diagnosis at

Figure 9.6. Equipment for nematode sampling: soil probe, bucket for mixing composite sample, sample bag, and replacement sand in watering can to fill sampling holes and aid in rapid recovery of the turf. (Courtesy R.L. Wick)

Figure 9.7. Filling sample holes with sand. (Courtesy R.L. Wick.)

the same time you submit a soil sample for nematodes. Obtain the sample prior to application of a nematicide.

The following is a general method for obtaining a nematode soil sample. However, prior to obtaining a sample, you should consult with the lab that will receive the sample as it is essential to follow their instructions for preparation and submission of samples.

1. Soil and roots should come from root zones of plants showing decline or at the outer margin of an affected area. Sampling from

dead plants provides little useful information for diagnostic purposes. For comparison, a second sample should be obtained from a healthy, adjoining area of turf.

2. Nematodes do not occur uniformly throughout the soil. Therefore, a composite sample of 15 to 20 cores (0.75–1 in. [2–2.5 cm] diameter) within 500 ft² (50 m²) should be obtained. Sample to a depth of 4 inches (10 cm), not including thatch. Each sample should amount to at least 1 cup (0.25 L).

3. Place sample in a plastic bag. The soil must be kept cool and moist or the nematodes will die. Do *not* add water to the sample. Label the *outside* of the bag; labels inside deteriorate rapidly.

4. Deliver the samples to a diagnostic lab as soon as possible along with the required information.

Interpretation of the Results

Since all soils contain nematodes, the diagnostic report will state the kinds and numbers of parasitic nematodes present. Nematode numbers are presented per volume — normally 100 cc, which is slightly more than 1/2 cup of soil. (See Table 9.1.)

The report will indicate whether the number for each nematode species exceeds local thresholds and justifies use of chemical control measures. Other considerations for deciding to use a nematicide would include aesthetic standards, budgets, and environmental concerns.

Periodic sampling during the growing season (3 to 4 times) may be recommended because nematode populations fluctuate over time. Each green can be considered a unique habitat due to differences in soil temperature, organic material, water holding capacity, microbes, and host plant composition. Also, each green may have a unique nematode species composition. For these reasons, a one-time comprehensive nematode assay can be very useful. If you assay all greens four times during the year, you will have the following information:

- Nematode species composition and seasonal fluctuation of each green. This is important for determining damage potential.
- Relative potential of each green to support nematode populations. Some will have environments conducive to high populations and others will not.

It is also useful to sample 4 to 6 weeks after a nematicide application to determine if the nematicide had an effect on the nematode population. Nematicides do not cause nematodes to disappear; they just make them stop feeding. It may take 4 to 6 weeks for the nematodes to die. Even when "contact" mortality occurs, the nematode is still extracted and counted in laboratory assays. An improved turf response is the best indication of whether nematodes were the primary cause of decline. However, a followup assay is advised, especially to determine if resistance has developed to a product or if the nematicide is being biologically degraded too quickly to be effective.

Develop a pest profile for each nematode! (See Chapter 2)

CULTURAL CONTROL STRATEGIES

Turfgrasses can withstand some feeding by most kinds of nematodes if the grass is healthy and stresses are minimal. Nematode management could be summarized as stress management, since minimizing other stresses will reduce the response of turf to nematodes and allow the grass to recover more quickly when attacked by nematodes. Refer to Chapter 8 on Disease Cultural Control Strategies.

- Irrigate properly; provide adequate water at the right time to encourage plant growth.
- Raise the mowing height to promote root and leaf growth so more carbohydrates can be produced in the leaves and then stored in the stems and roots.
- Provide adequate and balanced nutrition. Nutrient deficiencies can make turf more sensitive to root damage caused by nematodes.
- Learn when each nematode species is active in your region. Nematodes are more problematic during the summer in northern, temperate regions. In warmer climates, nematodes are active in the spring. Plan your control strategies accordingly.

Table 9.1. Common parasitic turfgrass nematodes.

Common Name/Genus	Cool-Season Turf*	Warm-Season Turf*
Awl (*Dolichodorus* spp.)	No	Yes (wet sites)
Cyst (*Heterodera* spp.)	Yes	Yes
Dagger (*Xiphinema* spp.)	Yes (ryegrass)	Yes (zoysiagrass)
Lance (*Hoplolaimus* spp.)	Yes (bentgrass, annual bluegrass)	Yes
Lesion (*Pratylenchus* spp.)	Yes	Yes
Needle (*Longidorus* spp.)	Yes	Yes
Pin (*Paratylenchus* spp.)	Yes (Kentucky bluegrass, fescues)	No
Ring (*Criconemella* spp.)	Yes	Yes (centipede)
Root-knot (*Meloidogyne* spp.)	Yes (bentgrass)	Yes (zoysiagrass)
Spiral (*Helicotylenchus* spp.)	Yes	Yes
Sting (*Belonolaimus* spp.)	No	Yes (sandy soils)
Stubby root (*Paratrichodorus* spp.)	Yes (Kentucky bluegrass, fescues)	Yes
Stunt (*Tylenchorhynchus* spp.)	Yes	Yes

*Grasses in parentheses are considered the most susceptible to this nematode.

BIOLOGICAL CONTROL STRATEGIES

Although nematologists have been working intensively in identifying potential biological control agents, no commercial biological controls are available. Laboratory and greenhouse studies have identified some promising agents, and work continues in this area. Promising organisms include bacteria, fungi, and non–plant-parasitic nematodes. Keep informed of research. In general, the organisms that have been identified as potential biocontrol agents inhibit only specific parasitic nematodes, and perhaps will work only in specific climatic conditions (Figures 9.8 and 9.9).

CHEMICAL CONTROL STRATEGIES

Pre-Plant Soil Fumigation

Soil fumigants are chemicals that produce gases, which diffuse through the soil. They are non-specific biocides, meaning that they will kill everything in the treated soil. To be effective, the soil fumigants must be applied correctly. Most fumigants are restricted-use pesticides that are applied by trained applicators with special licenses.

Fumigants have no residual effect. Nematodes that survive or escape treatment will initiate a new population in the soil. Also, vegetative grass material (e.g., bermudagrass sprigs) can introduce nematodes, especially if the nematodes are located inside the root at the time of introduction to the fumigated site.

Methyl bromide is a gas that is injected into the soil. The soil must be immediately covered with plastic to keep the gas from escaping. Because of its potential as an ozone-depleting chemical, this product is scheduled to be phased out of use in the next few years.

Chloropicrin/1,3-dichloropropene is a liquid soil fumigant (Telone C-17) that is injected into the soil, where it becomes a gas. Treated soil is covered with plastic to prevent the gas from escaping.

Metam-sodium (Vapam, Sectagon, Busan 1020) is a liquid soil fumigant that is either injected or drenched into the soil, where it becomes a gas. More effective control is obtained if the treated area is covered with plastic to prevent the gas from escaping.

Dazomet (Basamid) is a granular product that is incorporated into moist soil, where it becomes a gas. Again, more effective control is obtained if the treated area is covered with plastic to prevent the gas from escaping. This material should be uniformly incorporated into the root-zone mix to obtain the best results.

Post-Plant Chemical Control

Nematicides are chemicals applied to living turfgrass (Figure 9.10). No nematicide is effective against all nematodes. Furthermore, the effects of nematicides

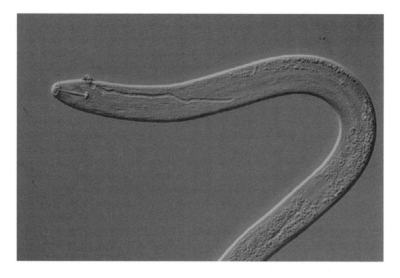

Figure 9.8. Nematode infected with a potential biocontrol fungus, *Hirsutella rhossiliensis*. (Courtesy B.A. Jaffee.)

Figure 9.9. Close-up of the head of a nematode recently infected by *Hirsutella rhossiliensis*. (Courtesy B.A. Jaffee.)

are temporary. Nematicides do not make turf grow new roots; they simply suppress the parasitic nematodes for a limited time period. If nothing is done to alleviate the other stresses on the plant, long-term effects from the nematicide will not be obtained.

It is critical that nematicides be applied correctly and at the appropriate time. For example, sting nematodes are most active in southern Florida on

Figure 9.10. Response of "Tifdwarf" bermudagrass to a nematicide (left) when applied in the spring when sting nematodes are active. (Courtesy M.L. Elliott.)

bermudagrass in the spring. Therefore, nematicide applications should be made at that time and not during the summer.

Nematicides do not necessarily kill nematodes, but may simply suppress them by temporarily paralyzing them. Materials registered for use as nematicides include:

- **fenamiphos** (Nemacur) — a systemic material.
- **ethoprop** (Mocap) — a non-systemic material; may be phytotoxic.

Do not overuse these materials:

- Nematodes least affected by the nematicide may increase in number and become the dominant population in the soil.
- Enhanced biodegradation of fenamiphos has been documented on golf courses in Florida, where the product has been used frequently. Enhanced biodegradation means that the repeated use of fenamiphos has encouraged the buildup of bacteria or fungi that can metabolize or degrade the chemical. They reduce the efficacy of the fenamiphos application because the longevity of the material in the soil is significantly reduced.
- These materials are toxic organophosphates. Exposure to humans and the environment should be minimized.
- Most nematicides are also broad-spectrum insecticides and have a detrimental effect on some beneficial insects, nematodes, and other fauna.

FURTHER READING

Davis, R.F., H.T. Wilkinson, and R.T. Kane. Nematodes in Creeping Bentgrass and Annual Bluegrass. *Golf Course Management*. 61(5):54–66, 1993.

Dernoeden, P.H. Symptomology and Management of Common Turfgrass Diseases in the Transition Zone and Northern Regions, in *Handbook of Integrated Pest Management for Turf and Ornamentals*, Leslie, A.R., Ed., Lewis Publishers, Boca Raton, FL, 1994.

Dropkin, V.H. *Introduction to Plant Nematology*. John Wiley & Sons, Inc., New York, NY, 1989.

Dunn, R.A. Nematode Management, in *Best Management Practices for Florida Golf Courses*. SP-141. Florida Cooperative Extension Service, Gainesville, FL, 1993.

Poinar, Jr., G.O., and R. Georgis. Biological Control for Plant-Parasitic Nematodes Attacking Turf and Ornamentals, in *Handbook of Integrated Pest Management for Turf and Ornamentals*, Leslie, A.R., Ed., Lewis Publishers, Boca Raton, FL, 1994.

Schumann, G.L. and J.D. MacDonald. *Turfgrass Diseases: Diagnosis and Management CD-ROM*. APS Press, St. Paul, MN, 1997.

Smiley, R.W., P.M. Dernoeden, and B.B. Clarke. *Compendium of Turfgrass Diseases*. APS Press, St. Paul, MN, 1992.

Todd, T.C. and N.A. Tisserat. Understanding Nematodes and Reducing Their Impact. *Golf Course Management*. 61(5):38–52, 1993.

Wick, R.L. Population Dynamics of Nematodes in Putting Greens. *Golf Course Management*. 57(3):100–112, 1989.

CHAPTER 10

PEST MANAGEMENT: WEEDS

On a golf course, as in any landscape, a weed is any plant other than the desired species. On some courses, annual bluegrass is managed or, perhaps, tolerated as a turfgrass, while on others it is considered a weed to be eliminated. Because weeds are plants, many of the same factors that affect the successful growth of turfgrass will favor weeds. However, most weeds are aggressive opportunists that can develop quickly in the appropriate environment. Thus, the best defense against weeds is a dense and healthy turfgrass sward that will compete against weed invasion. This is an excellent example of the importance of an *integrated* pest management program. Turfgrass areas that are poorly managed, or injured by insects, nematodes, or diseases, will be the same areas where weed encroachment is a problem (Figure 10.1).

GENERAL BIOLOGY

A few basic concepts about weed biology are helpful in identifying weeds, understanding their life cycles, predicting their activity, and determining appropriate control options. Most weeds are flowering plants that can be classified as broadleaf (dicotyledons) or grasses (monocotyledons). True grasses have hollow stems with nodes. Sedges and rushes are grass-like weeds that are a sub-group of monocots. Sedges have triangular, solid stems; rushes have round, solid stems. Weeds are also classified according to their life cycles:

Annual — completes life cycle from seed to plant to seed in one year (Figure 10.2).

Examples: henbit, smooth crabgrass, chickweed

Biennial — completes life cycle in two years, with flowering and seed production in the second year.

Examples: wild carrot, bull thistle

Perennial — may flower and produce seed each year, but also survives for three or more years by vegetative means such as rhizomes or tubers (Figures 10.3 and 10.4).

Examples: dandelion, clover, nutsedge, quackgrass

Figure 10.1. Weed encroachment. (Courtesy M.L. Elliott.)

Figure 10.2. Annual weed (*asiatic hawksbeard*). (Courtesy M.L. Elliott.)

In most cases, weeds have only one type of life cycle. However, annual bluegrass has developed two subspecies — winter annual and perennial. The seeds of the winter annual type require a dormancy period before germinating, whereas the perennial type has no dormancy requirement. It is common to have more than one type on your golf course.

Annual weeds are also classified according to when they complete their life cycle. Seed germination is primarily based on soil temperature and is the basis of accurate timing in the use of pre-emergence herbicides.

Figure 10.3. Perennial weed (false nutsedge) with rhizomes and seeds. (Courtesy M.L. Elliott.)

Figure 10.4. Perennial weed (yellow nutsedge) with rhizomes and tubers. See Color Plate 30. (Courtesy J.C. Neal.)

Winter annual weeds — complete life cycle from fall to spring.

Examples: chickweed, henbit, shepherd's purse, corn speedwell

Summer annual weeds — complete life cycle from spring to fall (Figure 10.5).

Examples: smooth crabgrass, goosegrass, pigweed, spurge, knotweed

Figure 10.5. Summer annual (Florida pusley). (Courtesy M.L. Elliott.)

KEY STEPS IN WEED MANAGEMENT

Identify the Weed

Turfgrass managers and IPM scouts should be able to identify each weed species that requires management. Some weeds are well known and easily identified (e.g., dandelion), but others are difficult to identify with certainty. Weeds may be difficult to identify at the immature stages, but this is the stage when they are most easily controlled. Unknown weeds should be observed until they reach a stage at which they can be identified in order to make appropriate future management decisions. Take pictures of the seedling and maturing plant and note the following characteristics for future reference.

- Broadleaf or grassy weed species
- Life cycle: annual, biennial, perennial
- Season, if annual: winter or summer
- Development stage: seedling, immature, mature

Map Established Weeds and Identify Weed Sources

Figure 10.6 shows a sample golf course weed map. As you map your course, note:

- Species of turfgrass and mowing height for each area
- Areas of thin, weak turfgrass
- Areas of weed encroachment:
  - weed species
  - abundance
  - patterns, e.g., along drainage patterns, shady areas, traffic areas

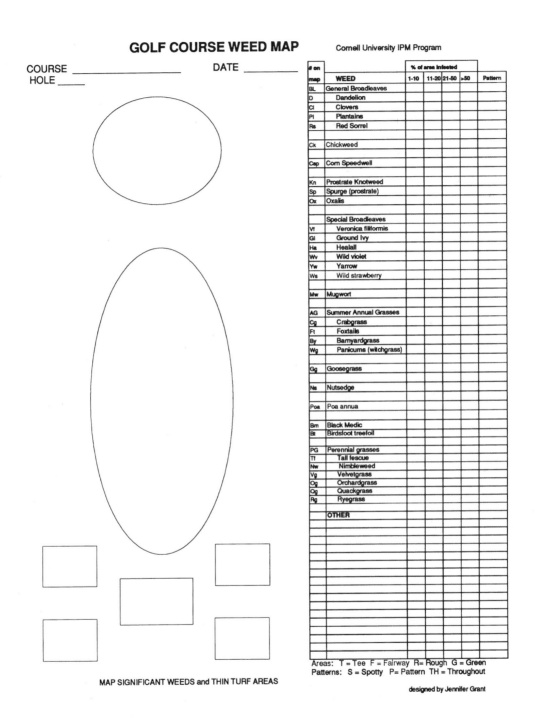

Figure 10.6. Sample golf course weed map. (Courtesy J.A. Grant, Cornell University.)

- Weed sources: topdressing materials, equipment, unmanaged neighboring meadows
- Areas of insect, nematode, or disease problems that could be future weed problem areas

Note Indicator Weeds

As plants, many weeds respond to the same environmental and cultural factors as turfgrass, requiring water, light, and nutrients. Certain weeds are very competitive with turfgrass when environmental factors are not optimal for turfgrass. Such weeds are called "indicators" because they indicate a turfgrass problem that requires correction. The following weeds are indicators of suboptimal environmental factors for turfgrass: (Figures 10.7 through 10.9)

Drought-Prone Sites
Annual lespedeza
Birdsfoot trefoil
Black medic
Bracted plantain
Goosegrass
Prostrate knotweed
Prostrate spurge
Yellow woodsorrel

Wet Sites
Alligator weed
Annual bluegrass
Sedges
Liverwort
Surface algae
Moss
Pearlwort
Rushes

Low-Nitrogen Fertility
Birdsfoot trefoil
Black medic
Broomsedge
Chicory
Common speedwell
Legumes in general (e.g., clover)
Quackgrass

High-Nitrogen Fertility
Annual bluegrass
Crabgrass
Chickweed
Ryegrass

Compacted Soil
Annual bluegrass
Annual sedge
Annual lespedeza
Broadleaf plantain
Corn speedwell
Goosegrass
Prostrate knotweed
Prostrate spurge

Infertile Sandy Soil
Poorjoe
Sandbur
Bracted plantain

Figure 10.7. Spotted spurge. (Courtesy M.L. Elliott.)

Figure 10.8. Globe sedge. (Courtesy M.L. Elliott.)

High Mowing Height/Infrequent
Bull thistle
Burdock
Chicory
Sweet clover
Teasel

Low Mowing Height/Frequent
Annual bluegrass
Chickweed
Pearlwort
Thymeleaf speedwell

Low-pH Soil
Red (sheep) sorrel

High-pH Soil
Plantain

Figure 10.9. White clover, flowering. (Courtesy J.C. Neal.)

Identify Causes of Poor Turfgrass Growth (Figure 10.10)

Growing Conditions:

- Environmental stresses: shade, poor air movement, poor drainage, pH extremes
- Physical damage: traffic patterns, divots, compaction
- Extreme weather conditions: ice, floods, hail, lightning, winter desiccation, heavy snow cover
- Pests: insects, diseases, nematodes, animal damage

Management Practices:

- Mowing: height, frequency, pattern
- Fertilizer: rate, timing, use of soil test information
- pH: soil, water
- Pesticide applications:
  - fungicides with growth regulator effects (e.g., sterol inhibitors)
  - plant growth regulator (PGR) applications
  - pesticides formulated as emulsifiable concentrates (EC) or other formulations that can cause phytotoxicity
- Aeration: type, depth, timing
- Drainage mechanisms
- Thatch management
- Traffic control

Careful observation of how these factors are affecting turfgrass growth and density will guide your choice of cultural strategies for weed management.

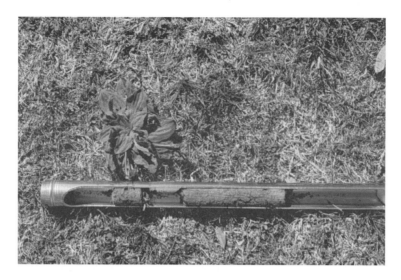

Figure 10.10. Compacted soil core on the left is from the weedy area with poorly growing turfgrass and a large infestation of broadleaf plantain. Soil core on the right is from a much less compacted area nearby with fewer weeds and better turf quality. See Color Plate 31. (Courtesy J.C. Neal.)

Weed Prevention

By preventing the introduction of weeds into an area, you eliminate the need to control the weeds. This is the most cost-effective and environmentally friendly way to control weeds.

At Time of Establishment:

- Use certified seed, sod, or sprigs to avoid planting weeds with turf-grass species.
- Plant turfgrass species and cultivars adapted to the region and to the type of use they will provide.
- Establish turf during conditions that are optimal for the species: fall for cool-season turfgrasses and spring for warm-season turfgrasses.
- Maintain sufficient moisture for germination, but avoid excess water, which favors turfgrass diseases and weakens the stand.
- Hand-pull weeds to reduce competition until turfgrass is established.
- If topsoil is introduced, be prepared to see many new weed species. Most will disappear after a few mowings, but scout these areas carefully to identify weeds that are difficult to control and remove them before they have a chance to spread.

In Established Turf:

- Maintain weed-free fences and pond/lake/ditch banks.

- Use clean, weed-free mulch and topdressing materials.
- Prevent weeds from producing seeds; NO SEEDS = NO WEEDS.

Develop a pest profile for each weed species! (See Chapter 2)

CULTURAL CONTROL STRATEGIES

Cultural strategies are most likely to provide a stable, long-term improvement in a turfgrass area. These strategies are designed to favor turfgrass growth and reduce the competitiveness of weeds.

Identification of the weeds that are successfully competing with the turfgrass species and knowledge of their life cycle are the first steps in determining which cultural control strategies are likely to be most successful (Figure 10.11).

- Aerate regularly to avoid excess thatch and soil compaction. Control traffic patterns to avoid wear and compaction.

  Examples: prostrate knotweed, prostrate spurge, goosegrass

- Avoid vertical cutting or cultivation (aeration) when annual weeds are germinating. If these procedures must be done at that particular time, use small-diameter tines to allow the turf to fill the holes more quickly.

  Examples: annual bluegrass, crabgrass

- Irrigate to avoid wilting of turfgrass, but do not overirrigate.

  Examples: Florida pusley, prostrate spurge

- Apply fertilizers to optimize turfgrass growth according to soil and leaf tissue test results, but avoid excess or deficient N. Use slow-release fertilizers or small, frequent applications of quick-release types. Apply N when weeds are not competitive.

  Examples: nimblewill (especially after frost when dormant), prostrate knotweed (in fall when in seed stage), crabgrass (early spring, before crabgrass germinates)

- Raise mowing height where indicator weeds are outcompeting turfgrass and when certain annual weed seeds are germinating. This will shade out the weed seedlings or prevent germination completely.

  Examples: during seed germination of annual bluegrass, crabgrass, dallisgrass

Figure 10.11. Creeping woodsorrel, a perennial turfgrass weed. (Courtesy J.C. Neal.)

- Lower height of cut and collect clippings when certain weeds are setting seed. Be sure to put clippings in a compost pile where the seeds will be killed.

  Examples: annual bluegrass, crabgrass, dallisgrass, quackgrass

- Pull certain weeds in small areas. It may be easier and more cost-effective than the use of chemical herbicides.

  Examples: dandelions, goosegrass, oxalis, Florida pusley; isolated patches of perennial weeds such as dallisgrass, nimblewill, tall fescue, orchardgrass, and Virginia buttonweed

> Pesticide usage at Panama Country Club is reduced because of member use of our "15th Club." The club is made from an old golf club shaft with a flail mower tip welded to it. Members, during play, see a weed and remove it. Some members have a goal to remove 5 weeds per round (Figure 10.12).
>
> — Jeff Ball, Golf Course Superintendent, Panama Country Club, Lynn Haven, Florida

BIOLOGICAL CONTROL STRATEGIES

There are no commercial biological controls available for turfgrass weeds at this time, but there is considerable research activity in the biocontrol of weeds. See Chapter 5 for further information (Figure 10.13).

Figure 10.12. Superintendent Jeff Ball removing a weed with the "15th Club."

CHEMICAL CONTROL STRATEGIES

When cultural control strategies fail to reduce weeds to an acceptable level and hand removal is impractical, chemical control may be necessary. It is imperative to know the tolerance of the desirable turfgrass species to the herbicides you may want to use (Figure 10.14).

Ways To Reduce Herbicide Use

- Spot-treat weed infestations.
- Apply herbicides when environmental conditions favor their efficacy. Time applications to avoid rain for *at least* 4 hours, and sometimes longer, depending on the herbicide (e.g., organic arsenicals). Be aware of temperature interactions with herbicides and desired turfgrass.
- Improved timing will help reduce the number of applications applied in a season. Pre-emergence herbicides will only be effective if applied prior to weed seed germination. Post-emergence herbicides should be applied when weeds are seedlings (2- to 4-leaf stage) and growing actively, or in the fall when established plants are better controlled.

Figure 10.13. A greenhouse biocontrol experiment using the fungus *Sclerotinia sclerotiorum* against plantain. See Color Plate 32. (Courtesy J.C. Neal.)

Figure 10.14. Leaf spot disease enhanced (on left) by the application of the herbicide MSMA. (Courtesy J.C. Neal.)

- Reduced rates of some herbicides may be effective, especially when combined with cultural practices. Check with local specialists for recommendations.
- Use of growth regulators along with cultural practices may be effective in annual bluegrass conversion programs. They can also be used to suppress seedhead formation, which improves the appearance and playability of the playing surface.

Types of Herbicides (See Table 10.1)

Non-Selective Herbicides

- In general, all plants that are sprayed with these herbicides will be killed or controlled. Glyphosate (Roundup) is a common example.
- Non-selective herbicides can be either contact (paraquat) or systemic (glyphosate).

Selective Herbicides

- These herbicides are able to control the targeted weed plant without seriously affecting the growth of the desired turfgrass. Their ability to do this is based on differential absorption, translocation, and morphological and/or physiological differences between the weed and the desired turfgrass. Most herbicides are selective.
- Selective herbicides can be either contact or systemic.

Contact Herbicides

- Only those plant parts that come in direct contact with the herbicide will be affected. Underground plant parts will not be affected. Repeat applications will be necessary to kill any regrowth from these underground plant parts.
- The weed foliage must be thoroughly covered for effective control. Plants are killed quickly (< 24 hours). Contact herbicides can be either selective or non-selective.

Systemic Herbicides

- These herbicides are absorbed by the plant and then translocated (moved) within the plant's vascular system. Therefore, underground parts are affected also. Because it may take days, or even weeks, for the herbicide to move throughout the plant, death of the targeted plant will take much longer than with contact herbicides.
- Systemic herbicides can be either selective or non-selective.

Pre-Emergence Herbicides

- These are herbicides that are applied *prior* to seed germination of targeted weed species. By forming a barrier at the soil surface, the emerging seedling's shoot or root tips come in contact with the herbicide.
- These are primarily used for control of annual weeds. Multiple applications are often necessary for season-long control, especially if more than one weed species is targeted.

- Since application timing is critical, you must plan ahead!
  - Which weed species do you want to control?
  - Do they all germinate at the same time?
  - When do the different weed species germinate?
- The use of degree-day models may make applications more precise (See Chapter 11 for specific examples). You do not want to apply too early, as the herbicide will start to degrade. Herbicide concentrations will decrease and so will efficacy.

Post-Emergence Herbicides

- These herbicides are applied to emerged weeds. In general, there is no soil residual activity.
- These may be used to control perennial or emerged annual weeds.
- Application timing is still critical. Weeds should be actively growing seedlings (2- to 4-leaf stage). This is especially true for contact-type herbicides. Larger weeds may require repeat applications.
- The turf should be actively growing also, so it can fill the voids the dead weeds leave behind. This means you must initiate a cultural control program *first* and be sure the turfgrass is not stressed before using herbicides.

Selecting an Herbicide

- **Efficacy on target weed species:** Determine what the local recommendations are, and read the herbicide labels.
- **Safety to turfgrass and the landscape** (non-target effects).
- **Application timing:** pre- or post-emergence; most programs will use both.
- **Speed of action:** contact vs. systemic.
- **Application method:** granules vs. spray.
- **Irrigation:** Can you follow the label directions?
- **Adjuvants:** Read the label carefully to determine if one is needed, especially surfactants or wetting agents, as most herbicides are formulated with an adjuvant. However, it may be necessary to add a buffering agent if your water pH is too high or too low.
- **Longevity of control:** Will the residue interfere with your turfgrass overseeding or turfgrass establishment program?
- **Mode and site of action:** How does the herbicide affect the target weeds? What is the location of herbicide activity within target weeds?
- **Chemical class:** Have you used this chemical class before? It is critical not to use the same chemical class repeatedly, as that can lead to development of resistance within the target weed species.

Table 10.1. Classes of selective herbicides.[a]

Chemical Class	Common Name	Trade Name (Example)	Mode of Action	Pre-Emergence	Post-Emergence
acetanilides	metolachlor	Pennant	inhibit root elongation	X(G[b])	
amides	pronamide	Kerb	mitotic poisons	X(G,B)	X(G)
	isoxaben	Gallery	cell wall synthesis inhibitor	X(B)	X(G)
aryl-oxy phenoxy	fenoxaprop	Acclaim	inhibit lipid metabolism		X(G)
	diclofop	Illoxan			X(G)
benzoic acids	dicamba	Banvel	plant growth regulator	X(B)	
benzothiadiazole	bentazon	Basagran	photosynthetic inhibitors		
cyclohexendiones	sethoxydim	Vantage	inhibit lipid metabolism		X(G,B)
	clethodim	Prism			X(G,B)
dinitroanilines	benefin	Balan	inhibit cell division	X(G)	
	oryzalin	Surflan		X(G,B)	
	pendimethalin	Pre-M, Pendulum, others			
	prodiamine	Barricade		X(G,B)	X((G,B)
imidazolinones	imazaquin	Image	disrupt protein synthesis	X(G,B)	X(G)
organic arsenicals	DSMA	Cleary's Methar 30	disrupt plant metabolism		X(G,B)
	MSMA	Daconate			X(G,B)
phenoxy acids	2,4-D		plant hormone mimics		X(B)
	dichlorprop/2,4-DP				X(G,B)
	MCPA				X(G,B)
	mecoprop/MCPP				X(G,B)
phenylureas	siduron	Tupersan	inhibits root growth	X(G)	

class	common name	trade name	mode of action		
phthalic acids	DCPA	Dacthal	inhibit cell division	X(G,B)	
pyridines	clopyralid	Confront (w/tridopyr)	plant hormone mimic		X(B)
	dithiopyr	Dimension	inhibits cell division	X(G,B)	X(B)
	triclopyr	Chaser, Turflon II (w/2,4-D)	plant growth regulator		X(B)
sulfonamides	bensulide	Betasan	inhibits cell division	X(G,B)	
sulfonylureas	chlorsulfuron	Lesco TFC	disrupt protein synthesis		X(G,B)
	halosulfuron	Manage			X(G,B)
triazines	metribuzin	Sencor	photosynthesis inhibitors	X(G,B)	X(G,B)
	simazine	Princep		X(G,B)	X(G,B)
not classified	oxadiazon	Ronstar	mitotic inhibitor		X(G)

[a] A number of herbicides are available in combinations for improved efficacy against a range of weed species. This chart lists only commonly used *selective* herbicides for use on established turf. Always read the labels for the specific recommendations of weed species controlled and turfgrass species tolerance and seeding information. *Non-selective* herbicides kill all plants and are used in areas where the turf will be reestablished after the weeds and previous turf have been eliminated.

[b] G= grassy weeds or sedges; B= broadleaf weeds.

Figure 10.15. Mouse-ear chickweed in a bentgrass approach. (Courtesy J.C. Neal.)

Resistance Management

As with all pesticides, repeated use of herbicides with the same mode of action may result in weed populations that are tolerant of or resistant to chemicals in that group. Resistance takes longer to develop with weeds that reproduce only once per year, compared to fungi and insects, which multiply more quickly. However, it is still important to prolong the usefulness of herbicides by rotation of active ingredients when possible, and to integrate herbicide use with cultural practices.

WEED IDENTIFICATION REFERENCES

Murphy, T.R., D.L. Colvin, R. Dickens, J.W. Everest, D. Hall, and L.B. McCarty. *Weeds of Southern Turfgrasses*. Alabama, Georgia, and Florida Cooperative Extension Services.

Scott's Guide to the Identification of Grasses, The Scotts Co. Marysville, OH.

Scott's Guide to the Identification of Dicot Weeds in Turf, The Scotts Co., Marysville, OH.

Stuckey et al. *Identifying Seedling and Mature Weeds in the Southeast.*, North Carolina State Agricultural Research Service, AG-208

USDA. *Common Weeds of the United States*. Dover Publications, Inc., NY, 1971.

Uva, R.H., J.C. Neal, and J.M. DiTomaso. *Weeds of the Northeast*. Cornell University Press, Ithaca, NY, (in press).

Weed Identification Guide. Southern Weed Science Society, Champaign, IL, 1990.

Whitson, T.D., L.C. Burrill, S.A. Dewey, D.W. Cudney, B.E. Nelson, R.D. Lee, and R. Parker. *Weeds of the West*. University of Wyoming, Laramie, WY, 1991.

Many states provide local identification guides and recommendations.

FURTHER READING

Baxendale, F.P. and R.E. Gaussoin, Eds. *Integrated Turfgrass Management for the Northern Great Plains.* Cooperative Extension, Institute of Agriculture and Natural Resources, University of Nebraska, Lincoln, NE, 1997.

Fermanian, T.W., M.C. Shurtleff, R. Randell, H.T. Wilkinson, and P.L. Nixon. *Controlling Turfgrass Pests.* Prentice-Hall, Inc., Upper Saddle River, NJ, 1997.

Johnson, B.J. Reduced Herbicide Application Rates: Crabgrass and Goosegrass Control in Bermudagrass. *TurfGrass Trends.* 5(1):1–6, 1996.

Johnson, B.J. and T.R. Murphy. Evaluating Reduced-Rate Herbicide Procedures. *Golf Course Management.* 63(2):150–154,156, 1995.

Murphy, T.R. Herbicide-Resistant Weeds in Turfgrasses. *TurfGrass Trends* 5(1):7–10, 1996.

Neal, J.C. 1996. Conducting a Bioassay for Herbicide Residues. *TurfGrass Trends* 5(1):11–12, 1996.

Neal, J.C. Turfgrass Weed Management — An IPM Approach, in *Handbook of Integrated Pest Management for Turf and Ornamentals*, Leslie, A.R., Ed., Lewis Publishers, Boca Raton, FL, 1994.

Watschke, T.L. Growth Regulators and *Poa annua. TurfGrass Trends.* 5(3):1–4, 1996.

Watschke, T.L., P.H. Dernoeden, and D.J. Shetlar. *Managing Turfgrass Pests.* Lewis Publishers, Boca Raton, FL, 1995.

Watschke, T.L. and J.M. DiPaola. 1995. Plant Growth Regulators. *Golf Course Management.* 63(3):59–62.

CHAPTER 11

DEVELOPING TECHNOLOGIES FOR PEST MANAGEMENT

PEST PREDICTION MODELS

Plant Phenology

Plant development is easy to observe, but similar patterns occur for all life forms, including the pests and pathogens of turfgrass. The concept is familiar to anyone who has observed that plants tend to break bud, bloom, and set fruit at a fairly predictable time and order each season. When temperatures are below normal, development is delayed; when temperatures are above normal, development speeds up and people speak of an "early spring." For many years, pesticides have been applied according to certain stages of plant development because plants, insects, and all life forms are affected by temperature. Thus, plant phenology (stage of development) reflects the appropriate stage of development for a turfgrass pest, and is much easier to discern than the development of tiny pests such as insects.

Examples: Application of a pre-emergent crabgrass herbicide when bridal wreath spirea (*Spiraea X. Vanhouttei*) blooms.

Application of insecticides for annual bluegrass weevil and black turfgrass ataenius adults during the period between forsythia full bloom and dogwood (*Cornus florida*) full bloom.

Degree-Days

Degree-days are a method used to quantify the accumulation of heat units during a growing season. It is a method of more accurately measuring the seasonal development that is witnessed in plant phenology.

Figure 11.1 shows how temperature affects the development of a living organism. There is a minimum threshold temperature, below which the organism cannot develop, as well as a maximum threshold temperature, above which it cannot develop or dies.

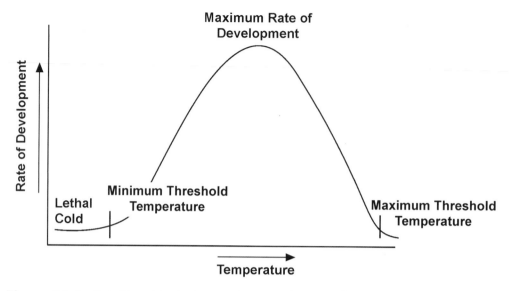

Figure 11.1. Relationship between temperature and organism development.

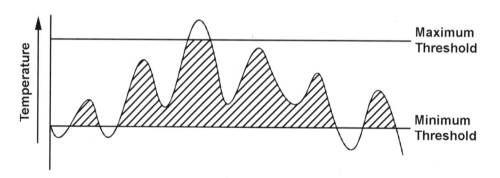

Figure 11.2. Calculation of degree-days.

Calculation of Degree-Days

Degree-days are determined by calculating the shaded area in Figure 11.2, which is the amount of time the temperature is *above* the minimum threshold temperature and *below* the maximum threshold temperature. A precise calculation of degree-days requires complex mathematics to determine the shaded area. However, a close estimate of degree-days can be calculated more simply in the following way:

1. Calculate the average temperature for each day:
   (daily maximum temperature + daily minimum temperature) divided by 2
2. Subtract the "base" (minimum threshold) temperature from the average temperature for that day. The base temperature varies with each organism.

If the average daily temperature is *less* than the base temperature, *zero* degree-days are accumulated, but none are subtracted from the total. If the average daily temperature is *more* than the base temperature, the difference is added to the total.

This technique is not as precise as some of the more complicated systems used by researchers, but it is adequate for most situations encountered by golf course superintendents. Furthermore, it only requires a min/max thermometer.

Example: Degree-day accumulation for an organism with a base temperature of 50°F

	Temperature			Degree-Days
	maximum	minimum	average	
1 May	60	40	50	0 (average = base)
2 May	70	40	55	5 (average > base)
3 May	70	50	60	10 (average > base)
4 May	50	40	45	0 (average < base)
			Total degree days =	15

Researchers make observations on pest development to determine the correlation between the number of degree-days and when control measures need to be initiated. Such information can greatly improve the precision of chemical and biocontrol applications, particularly in unusually warm or cool years. It can reduce the repeated applications of pesticides that sometimes occur when superintendents are not sure of the developmental stage of a pest.

Several commercial systems have the capacity to calculate degree-days, including:

Network 8000 Automatic Irrigation System (The Toro Company, Irrigation Division, Riverside, California)

EnviroCaster (Neogen Corporation, Lansing, Michigan) (Figures 11.3 and 11.5)

Metos Golf (Gempler's Inc., Mt. Horeb, Wisconsin) (Figure 11.4)

We use IPM techniques to avoid disease problems by not overwatering. We use a personal computer/central controller and an on-site weather station. We avoid diseases from overwatering since this system allows us to apply only the amount of water the turf needs, and we can apply it in intervals, which avoids runoff and puddling. Local soil temperatures from the university weather network (AZMET) give us information on when to apply pre-emergent herbicides. We get better weed control this way.

— Peter Hill, CGCS, La Poloma Country Club, Tucson, Arizona

Figure 11.3. EnviroCaster Weather Station. (Courtesy G.L. Schumann.)

Figure 11.4. Metos Golf Weather Station. (Courtesy T. Green.)

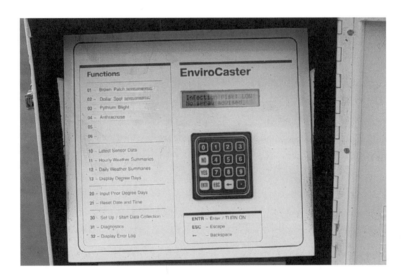

Figure 11.5. EnviroCaster control panel. (Courtesy G.L. Schumann.)

Insect Examples

Annual Bluegrass Weevil (*Listronotus maculicollis*):

A degree-day model predicts optimum timing of application for the second generation. The model uses a baseline air temperature of 50°F (10°C) and recommends an accumulation of 1,000 to 1,150 degree-days as the threshold for optimum timing of insecticide application.

Limitation: The model has not been validated in the field.

Black Turfgrass Ataenius (*Ataenius spretulus*):

A degree-day model predicts when egg laying will occur for both the first and second generation.

Limitation: The model has not been validated in the field.

Bluegrass Billbug (*Sphenophorus parvulus*):

A degree-day model predicts when each stage will be present. Using a March 1 starting date and a baseline temperature of 50°F (10°C), first adult activity should occur between 280 and 352 degree-days. The 30% first activity level (the time that the last surface insecticide would be effective) should occur between 560 and 624 degree-days.

Limitation: Often, more than one billbug species is present in a given area, and each appears to require a different model.

Sod Webworms (several species):

Degree-day models exist for at least two species (larger sod webworm, *Pediasia trisecta*, and bluegrass webworm, *Parapediasia teterrella*), predicting adult flight activity.

Limitation: The model has not been validated in the field.

Masked Chafers (*Cyclocephala* spp.):

Degree-day models (coupled with rainfall patterns) predict adult flight activity for both northern and southern masked chafers.

Limitation: The model has not been validated in the field.

See pages 190 and 191 for general limitations to prediction systems.

Disease Examples

Root Diseases

Timing of preventive applications of fungicides for root diseases such as summer patch is difficult. Soil temperatures have been used as an indicator of initial activity of the fungi in the soil, but degree days have the potential to determine the optimal time for application more accurately. It is likely that soil moisture will also be an important predictive factor. No specific recommendations are currently available.

Initial Fungicide Applications

Degree-days might also be an indicator for initial fungicide applications for certain diseases. This is most likely to be useful in areas where soil must warm up following winter conditions. No specific recommendations have been developed yet.

Weed Examples

Annual Bluegrass Seedhead Prediction

This model has been developed for use in northern areas where the annual bluegrass has a dormant period each winter (not to be used in southern or westerns areas of the United States). It is a degree-day model based on a baseline soil temperature of 50°F (10°C). It reports seedhead formation before they are visible to help with the timing of the application of the growth regulator mefluidide. There is generally a 4- to 8-day "window" for effective application. The model is available in the EnviroCaster by Neogen Corporation, which recommends an accumulation of 50 degree-days as the threshold for best control.

Crabgrass Germination for Timing of
Pre-Emergent Herbicide Application

This model uses a fixed calendar date of April 1 to begin accumulating degree-days, which should apply to the mid-Atlantic and northern states. Emergence was first observed at 42–78 degree days with a 73°F (22.8°C) soil temperature baseline at 1 in. (2.5 cm) depth.

ENVIRONMENTAL MONITORING FOR
DISEASE PREDICTION AND CONTROL

Nearly all of the fungi that cause common turfgrass diseases are already present in established turfgrasses. They are too small to observe or count easily, so most disease prediction is accomplished by monitoring the environmental factors that allow pathogens to infect the turf and favor disease development. The most important environmental factors are water and temperature. These are monitored in a variety of forms, including:

- Leaf wetness
- Relative humidity (RH)
- Rainfall/irrigation
- Soil moisture
- Solar radiation
- Temperatures (minimum, maximum, mean)
  – air
  – soil
- Wind speed and direction

The disease prediction systems currently available are all for foliar diseases of cool-season turfgrasses: anthracnose, brown patch, dollar spot, and Pythium blight. Although superintendents are already predicting disease based on their own experience and the history of their golf course, disease prediction systems developed by researchers may make fungicide application decisions more precise and reduce applications when conditions approach — but do not quite reach — those needed for a severe disease outbreak.

> We purchased the GroWeather monitoring system from Davis Industries in Hayward, California. Using the information from the Growing Degree System, we will be able to optimize the timing of our chemical applications and have data to justify it. It is downloaded into a computer for a hard copy. We will develop models for our course. It is another less expensive option to make educated decisions.
>
> — Michael Gunn, Golf Course Superintendent, Wahconah Country Club, Dalton, Massachusetts

Disease Prediction Models May Be Based On:

Infection Periods

A prediction is made each time the required environmental conditions necessary for disease initiation occur. Infection or penetration of a turfgrass plant by a pathogen does not necessarily mean that disease will develop. This system is useful for diseases that may be severe and develop rapidly.

Pythium Blight:

Example 1: The traditional "150 Rule" recommends fungicide applications whenever relative humidity (RH) + temperature (°F) ≥ 150.

Example 2: Prediction factors for severe disease are temperature [maximum >86°F (30°C), and minimum >68°F (20°C)] and at least 14 hr RH >90% in the previous 24 hours for severe disease.

Example 3: Prediction factors are temperature ≥ 70°F (21°C) for more than 18 hours. If minimum temperature in the previous 24 hr was >68°F (20°C), then high risk for disease is predicted. If minimum temperature is ≤ 68°F (20°C), moderate risk for disease is predicted.

Brown Patch: (see Chapter 2 and references at end of this chapter)

Severity Factors

Environmental conditions are given a point value depending on how favorable they are for disease. A control recommendation is offered once the points accumulate to a threshold number. A severity factor prediction system is useful for less severe diseases that do not always require fungicide control, such as anthracnose, red thread, and leaf spot. An added advantage is that the threshold can be modified for the local conditions and disease tolerance of a particular site, which is an excellent application of IPM theory.

Anthracnose Severity Index (ASI):

Prediction factors are based on hours of leaf wetness (**L**) and average daily temperature (**T**).

- Hours of leaf wetness (L)
- Average daily temperature (T)

Points are accumulated daily using this equation:

$$ASI = 4.0233 - 0.2283L - 0.5308T - 0.0013L^2 + 0.0197T^2 + 0.0155LT$$

Infection can occur whenever ASI >2. This model can be used to accumulate points up to a predetermined threshold based on local conditions. A computer can make the calculations daily.

Uses of Prediction Models

- Timing of first fungicide application.
- Timing of re-applications, especially if pathogen level can be monitored (e.g., through immunoassays described in next section).
- Timing of biocontrol applications (which may remain effective for only short periods of time).
- Management of other pests that can be predicted by environmental monitoring, e.g., insects, weeds.
- Predicting availability of slow-release fertilizers.

Current Limitations of Prediction Models

- **Historical weather data** are the basis for predictions. The favorable environmental factors have already occurred. If a fungicide is necessary, it must usually be applied the same day as the prediction, which may be difficult to schedule at some courses.

- **Infection vs. disease:** If environmental conditions change quickly and become less favorable, disease may not develop even though infection has occurred. One brown patch prediction system cancels predictions if temperatures fall below 59°F (15°C) in the 48 hr following the message.
- **Regional accuracy:** Prediction models are usually developed in one area and are then subjected to limited testing. Test new systems on an experimental area to be sure that they are accurate for your local conditions.
- **Oversimplification:** Disease events occur because of a complex interaction of factors. Early models were kept very simple so they would not impose time-consuming calculations on busy turfgrass managers. Computers allow models to become more complex, and hopefully more accurate, while not requiring complex calculations on the part of the manager.
- **Accuracy requires on-site data:** Environmental data recorded even at a neighboring course may not be appropriate for your golf course. The site of an environmental monitoring unit is important. Some turf managers choose to place them in the most disease-prone areas for early warnings; others prefer a more "average" location. For convenience and safety, units are often placed near the operations building. However, be sure the unit is placed where it will not be sheltered from the environment it is expected to monitor.
- **Other factors,** besides the environment, affect infection and disease severity. These include:

  - turfgrass species and cultivar
  - use of chemical growth regulators
  - nitrogen fertility (and other nutrients)
  - soil factors
  - pesticide use
  - pathogen variability

As future models become more complex, they will include these factors in addition to the current environmental data.

- **Duration of fungicide activity:** Prediction systems notify you each time the environmental conditions are right for infection. Once a fungicide has been applied, you may ignore future predictions during the time the fungicide remains effective. As you approach the end of the application interval, you must begin to monitor for new predictions. In the future, it may be possible to monitor fungicide residues to determine exactly how long an application remains active using developing technologies (including immunoassays described in the next section).

Commercial Disease Prediction Devices

EnviroCaster — Neogen Corporation, 620 Lesher Place, Lansing, MI 48912; (1-800-234-5333)
Environmental sensors: air and soil temperatures, leaf wetness, rainfall, relative humidity, soil moisture, wind speed and direction
Models: degree-days, anthracnose, brown patch, Pythium blight, annual bluegrass seedhead production

Metos Golf — from Gottfried Pessl, Austria — available in the U.S. through Gempler's, Inc., P.O. Box 270, Mt. Horeb, WI 53572 (1-800-272-7672)
Environmental sensors: air and soil temperatures, day length, leaf wetness, rainfall, relative humidity, soil moisture, solar radiation, wind speed and direction
Models: degree-days, evapotranspiration, brown patch, dollar spot, Pythium blight

RAPID DISEASE IDENTIFICATION

If a disease cannot be diagnosed with certainty based on symptoms and observation of active mycelia, a diagnostician should be consulted. Unfortunately, this requires delivery of the sample and at least an overnight wait for the results. A new technology offers rapid identification of some diseases on site in about 10 minutes. Antibody tests, or immunoassays, use antibodies produced by the immune systems of animals for plant pathogen identification. The antibodies can be produced by tissue culture for commercial uses. When the appropriate pathogen is detected, a color change can be easily observed because the antibodies are linked to an enzyme that causes a chemical reaction resulting in color development. Such tests are called ELISA tests (*enzyme-l*inked *i*mmuno-*sorbent a*ssays). They have many applications, including home pregnancy tests.

Commercial antibody tests — immunoassays (Figures 11.6 and 11.7) are available for:

- Brown patch
- Dollar spot
- Pythium blight (may be useful for Pythium root rot if a very clean root sample is used)

Alert kits from Neogen Corporation, 620 Lesher Place, Lansing, MI 48912 (1-800-234-5333)

Antibody tests in development by researchers:

- Necrotic ring spot
- Summer patch
- Other ectotrophic root-infecting fungi

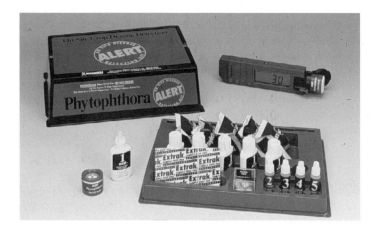

Figure 11.6. Alert immunoassay field kits can be used for rapid disease diagnosis in the field. (Courtesy Neogen Corporation.)

Figure 11.7. Completing an immunoassay identification. (Courtesy Neogen Corporation.)

Some *advantages* of the kits are:

- They offer identification of a specific pathogen.
- The test is fast (10 minutes).
- The test can be done anywhere; sterile conditions are not necessary. However, avoid soil and thatch in the sample, which may give false positive readings.

Some *disadvantages* of the kits are:

- A different kit is needed for each disease.
- Antibody kits are composed of proteins that must be refrigerated between uses, and must not be frozen or exposed to high temperatures.
- Kits expire after about 9 months.

Quantifying the Results

You can roughly judge the amount of pathogen detected by observing the color development. A light color indicates that little pathogen was detected. A dark spot indicates that more pathogen has been detected. A meter is available that will quantify the color density with a number that is useful for IPM recordkeeping. Interpretation of these numbers is somewhat difficult in the absence of symptoms. In turfgrass where the pathogen is active, but disease symptoms are not yet visible, a wide range of results can be obtained.

Some turf managers use the meter readings *as one tool* in making fungicide application decisions. Others use the kits primarily as an identification guide.

Combining Immunoassays With Environmental Prediction Systems

Environmental prediction systems only tell you that the conditions are conducive for disease development. Immunoassays can provide you with the additional information that the fungus is present and active. This is particularly useful as you approach the end of a fungicide application interval and are not sure if the fungicide is still present at a level that will prevent disease.

HOODED SPRAYERS

Hooded sprayers help prevent drift of liquid pesticide applications (Figure 11.8). They allow application of pesticides in windier weather than conventional sprayers can handle. Because they reduce drift, hooded sprayers might be a better choice when applying pesticides in environmentally sensitive areas, such as along edges of ponds. Hooded sprayers also reduce exposure of the applicator to pesticide drift during application.

SUBSURFACE PLACEMENT OF PESTICIDES

Subsurface applications of pest control products began with the use of soil fumigation equipment for plant-parasitic nematode control. Today, rapidly expanding technology provides opportunities to place control products below the turf surface for soil insect control.

Advantages:

• Places product closer to pest.
• Removes pesticides from exposure to surface light and heat.
• Reduced surface residues means less exposure to people/wildlife.
• Reduced drift.
• In some cases, reduced rates work as well as full surface-applied rates.

Figure 11.8. Hooded pesticide sprayer. (Courtesy P.J. Vittum.)

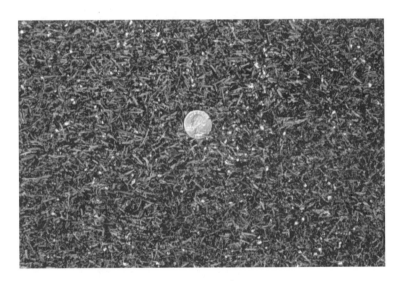

Figure 11.9. Surface application of granular pesticides may result in unacceptable exposure of humans and other non-target species. (Courtesy P.J. Vittum.)

- Can be contracted to commercial applicators; therefore, no equipment upkeep for golf course.

Disadvantages:

- Not all products work well as subsurface applications.
- Most equipment is expensive or highly specialized.
- Product labelling is questionable for subsurface placement in some states with some products.
- Equipment versatility for other tasks is usually low.

Most subsurface applications are done by contract commercial applicators, particularly for mole cricket control in the southeastern United States. Recent technology promises less expensive, more versatile equipment that is easier and less expensive to maintain.

Extension specialists and turf product suppliers in your area usually know sources for equipment purchase or contract application. Some contract applicators will bid on treatment of mapped areas rather than "wall-to-wall" applications.

Slicing Applications

Granules

Granules are applied below the surface using applicators that cut furrows into which the granules drop. Most operate in a manner similar to overseeders. Cuts are made by a series of knives, spikers, or discs. Furrows are then closed after the granules drop (Figures 11.10 and 11.11).

Advantage:

• Depth of delivery can be adjusted very precisely.

Disadvantages:

• Application may be slower than conventional applicators.
• Some cutting devices can disrupt the playing surface, leaving visible marks.

Formulations Applied in Water

Equipment is similar to the subsurface granular placement (described above). Liquids flow at low pressure (usually no more than 40 psi, and sometimes by gravity flow) into furrows cut by colters.

Advantages:

• Can be used to apply biological control products (e.g., entomopathogenic nematodes).
• Does not involve high pressures (and the dangers inherent in high pressures).

Disadvantages:

• Application may be slower than conventional applications.
• Some cutting devices can disrupt the playing surface, leaving visible marks.

Figure 11.10. Subsurface pesticide applicator for granules. (Courtesy P.P. Cobb.)

Figure 11.11. Close-up of applicator. (Courtesy P.P. Cobb.)

High-Pressure Liquid Injection Applications

High-pressure liquid applicators (Figures 11.12 and 11.13) generate pressures up to 5,000 psi (27,500 kPa). Applications are made by injecting liquids directly into the turf and/or soil. Nozzles are placed just above the ground (usually no more than 0.5 in./1.25 cm), sometimes over a drag bar, and force liquids below the surface. Pressure alone drives the spray material directly into the soil. Depth of penetration is determined by the pressure generated, the ground speed at which the unit is operated, soil moisture conditions, soil texture, and amount of thatch.

Figure 11.12. High-pressure liquid (HPL) injection applicator. (Courtesy P.P. Cobb.)

Figure 11.13. Close-up of an HPL nozzle drag bar. (Courtesy P.J. Vittum.)

Advantages:

- Most systems do not disrupt the playing surface.
- Some systems can apply insecticides nearly as rapidly as comparable conventional surface application systems.

Disadvantages:

- Potential hazards inherent in using very high pressures.
- Cannot be used to apply some biological control organisms.

RAPID FOLIAR NUTRIENT MONITORING

Determining the exact amount of fertilizer needed to optimize the growth of turfgrass has always been something of a guessing game. Soil test results and tissue test results are important guides. Superintendents must also monitor rainfall, temperature, and other factors that affect turfgrass growth. The role of nutrients on disease development is well known, especially with regard to nitrogen levels. Many foliar diseases are known as "low-nitrogen" or "high-nitrogen" diseases. A number of superintendents are now "spoon feeding" fertilizers — some with fertigation — to provide sufficient nutrients for good turfgrass growth without adding excessive levels that can lead to disease outbreaks. Traditional laboratory nutrient analyses of tissue and soil are time-consuming and cost money for each sample analyzed.

A technology, first developed for forage testing, is being investigated for its use in rapid and frequent monitoring of turfgrass clippings. The device uses near infrared reflectance spectroscopy (NIRS) of dried turfgrass clipping samples to give an assessment of macro- and micronutrients in a matter of minutes.

The analysis requires clean, dry samples of turfgrass clippings. The clippings can be dried overnight in a drying oven or more quickly using a microwave oven. The clippings are then run through a mill to produce a fine powder and placed in a quartz glass disc (Figure 11.14). The disc is placed in the NIRS machine, which produces near-infrared light (Figure 11.15). The spectrophotometer directs a beam of near-infrared light onto the sample. The reflected wavelength is calculated with computer equations designed for various turfgrass species to predict nitrogen and 15 other chemical constituents (primarily macronutrients and micronutrients) of the turfgrass. The results are displayed on the computer monitor. Reports can be stored in computer files and/or printed out.

This technology requires further evaluation by researchers to determine:

- Correlation between traditional lab analysis and NIRS analysis.
- Optimal foliar nutrient levels.
- Optimal balance between nutrients.
- Target values for different turfgrass species.

Some superintendents process their own samples on their own machines, while others use a service provided by a consultant who maintains the device and processes the samples with a rapid reporting system.

Commercial near-infrared reflectance spectrophotometers are available from:

BioPro, The Toro Co., Bloomington, Minnesota (908-722-9830)
Turf Analyzer, Karsten Turf, P.O. Box 82818, Phoenix, Arizona 85071-2818 (602-870-5598)

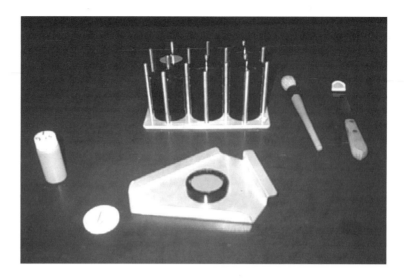

Figure 11.14. Dried and milled clippings are prepared for near-infrared spectro-photometric (NIRS) analysis. (Courtesy G.L. Schumann.)

Figure 11.15. Karsten NIRS foliar nutrient analyzer and computer. (Courtesy G.L. Schumann.)

Without question, the most accomplished and successful turf managers are individuals who never lose sight of the basics, yet implement new technologies that promote sound agronomic practices. IPM is the marriage of old and new management practices that results in high quality turf and responsible environmental stewardship. IPM is a comprehensive management method that works!

— Ronald E. Milenski, CGCS, The International, Bolton, Massachusetts

FURTHER READING

Burpee, L.L. and L.G. Goulty. Evaluation of Two Dollarspot Forecasting Systems for Creeping Bentgrass. *Canadian Journal of Plant Science*. 66:345–351, 1986.

Danneberger, T.K., B.E. Branham, and J.M. Vargas. Mefluidide Applications for Annual Bluegrass Seedhead Suppression Based on Degree-Day Accumulation. *Agronomy Journal*. 79:69–71, 1987.

Danneberger, T.K. and J.M. Vargas. Annual Bluegrass Seedhead Emergence as Predicted by Degree-Day Accumulation. *Agronomy Journal*. 76:756–758, 1984.

Danneberger, T.K., J.M. Vargas, and A. Jones. A Model for Weather-Based Forecasting of Anthracnose on Annual Bluegrass. *Phytopathology*. 74:448–451, 1984.

Dara, S.T. Turf Tissue Testing: Challenges, Approaches, and Recommendations. *Golf Course Management*. 96(3):63–66, 1996.

Dinelli, D. Weather Stations. *Golf Course Management*. 63(4):26–36, 1995.

Fidanza, M.A. and P.H. Dernoeden. Evaluation of an Enzyme-Linked Immunosorbent Assay Method for Predicting Brown Patch Infection in Turf. *HortScience*. 30:1263–1265, 1995.

Fidanza, M.A., P.H. Dernoeden, and A.P. Grybauskas. Development and Field Validation of a Brown Patch Warning Model for Perennial Ryegrass Turf. *Phytopathology*. 86:385–390, 1996.

Fidanza, M.A., P.H. Dernoeden, and M. Zhang. Degree-Days for Predicting Smooth Crabgrass Emergence in Cool-Season Turfgrasses. *Crop Science*. 36:990–996, 1996.

Gelernter, W.D. Insect Degree-Day Models for Turf. *Golf Course Management*. 64(1):63–72, 1996.

Happ, K. Tissue Testing: Questions and Answers. *USGA Green Section Record* 32(4):9–11, 1994.

Hall T.J., L.V. Madden, and D.J. McCormick. Forecasting Turfgrass Diseases — An Update. *Golf Course Management*. 53:74–78, 1985.

Nutter, F.W., H. Cole, Jr., and R.D. Schein. Disease Forecasting System for Warm Season Pythium Blight of Turfgrass. *Plant Disease*. 67:1126–1128, 1983.

Orton, D.A. Using Plants to Time Pest Control. *Grounds Maintenance*. 31(4)14–19, 1996.

Orton, D.A. *Coincide: The Orton System of Pest Management*. Plantsmen's Publications, Flossmoor, IL, 60422.

Schumann, G.L., B.B. Clarke, L.V. Rowley, and L.L. Burpee. Use of Environmental Parameters and Immuno-Assays to Predict Rhizoctonia Blight and Schedule Fungicide Applications on Creeping Bentgrass. *Crop Protection*. 13:211–218, 1994.

Shane W.W. Use of Disease Models for Turfgrass Management Decisions, in *Handbook of Integrated Pest Management for Turf and Ornamentals*, Leslie, A.R., Ed., Lewis Publishers, Boca Raton, FL, 1994.

Shane, W.W. Prospects for Early Detection of Pythium Blight by Antibody-Aided Monitoring of Pythium Blight on Turfgrass. *Plant Disease*. 75:921–925, 1991.

Shetlar, D. Predicting Insect Patterns Via Weather Cycles. *Lawn and Landscape Maintenance*. 68(4):70–72, 1991.

Vittum, P.J. Enhanced Efficacy of Isazophos Against Japanese Beetle (Coleoptera: Scarabacidae) Grubs Using Subsurface Placement Technology. *Journal of Economic Entomology*. 87:162–167, 1994.

Vittum, P.J. High Pressure Injection for White Grub Control. *Golf Course Management*. 57(11):46–48, 1989.

Wilkinson, H.T. and D. York. Foliar Test for Turf Nutrients. *Grounds Maintenance*. 61(7):24–28, 66, 1993.

CHAPTER **12**
GETTING STARTED

SETTING GOALS

Some people expect to set goals for next year, but forget that you first have to get through this week and this month. Both long-term and short-term goals are needed, and both need to be realistic. You should always know what expectations the golfers, course owner, and your staff have of you and the facility you manage. Likewise, they should be aware of your expectations. Here are some tips and examples to help you set goals:

Short-Term Goals

Tip:
Concentrate on real, immediate needs. Be realistic; use available resources and set priorities.

Examples:
Set thresholds and determine monitoring tasks, not for *all* pests, but for your *most important* (damage and/or costs). Decide who will be involved in setting the thresholds.

Determine priority areas and examine current management practices for these areas. Correct or alter practices where necessary. Include soil tests and irrigation system checks where needed.

Don't have a weather station and can't afford one? Buy a min/max thermometer, a rain gauge, and a soil temperature probe. Then monitor *every day* and record.

Develop job descriptions for scout; develop record sheets.

Get help training a scout before the prime growing season. Once a scout is trained and experienced, that scout can train another.

Figure 12.1. Short-term goal: Remove or thin trees. (Courtesy P.P. Cobb.)

Apply chemical controls only when thresholds have been reached, and according to label directions.

Evaluate results of management changes and control strategies; make adjustments where necessary.

Start an IPM resource file.

Pull 20 weeds daily from weedy area.

Long-Term Goals

Tip:
Be realistic
and imaginative.

Examples:
Two years from now we will have reduced insect damage on greens by 50% through scouting and proper timing of controls.

Identify areas where weeds are a major problem and determine the underlying cause.

Expand the use of native or well-adapted plants in out-of-play areas.

Begin to retrofit the irrigation system.

Increase scouting program to include approaches by next year.

Figure 12.2. Long-term goal: Map all the fairways for weeds. (Courtesy P.P. Cobb.)

Save enough money in 3 years on pesticide expenses to purchase a weather station (unless money is available for purchase as a short-term goal).

Establish non-host plantings for reduced pest pressure in sensitive areas.

Reduce need for herbicide use on fairways by increasing the health and vigor of the turf.

Renovate areas where drainage problems exist.

Long-term goals can be reached only by achieving the daily, weekly, and monthly goals. You will not develop an extensive IPM program within a day or even a year. Because management practices, environmental conditions, pest populations, and clientele change, short-term goals may also vary.

- **Start small and build on what you are already doing successfully.**

- **Expand your program as you learn.**

- **What do you think you should achieve in the next five years?**

Who Should Set The Goals?

Those persons who are decision makers are usually responsible for setting goals. However, each person involved in an activity will probably have some input. Those who are ultimately responsible for the outcome need to have a major role in formulating these goals and developing a plan. Involve management, golfers, and staff in establishing goals.

Figure 12.3. Careful daily observations are valuable. (Courtesy G.L. Schumann.)

Remember:

- *Write it down.* Start by describing where you are now and where you hope to go. Develop a realistic plan within the context of your budget and available staff. Include short- and long-term goals. Don't plan or promise more than you can deliver!
- *Involve management and staff* in the planning stage.

POLICY STATEMENTS

IPM is a common sense approach that includes managing pests. You need a written plan as well as goals. Policy statements should document:

- Your "mission statement" or overall rationale — your reasons for an IPM approach.
- Goals (short- and long-term).
- How you plan to achieve the goals.
- What resources you have and what you need.
- List of start-up costs, both in time and actual dollars.
- How you think this effort will impact the golf course and the community.

Introductory Information

- Overall philosophy toward turf management. Define IPM in terms your audience can understand.
- Needs and expectations of the golfers and potential conflicts with IPM philosophy.
- Particular conditions that make turf management challenging at certain locations.

General Maintenance Goals (Examples)

- Priority areas (usually in this order: greens, tees, fairways, roughs)
- Drainage issues
- Irrigation issues
  - delivery system
  - water supply
  - water quality
- Renovation issues
  - new or larger greens
  - altering or amending soil profile
  - altering turfgrass species or cultivars
  - tree removal or pruning
  - traffic patterns

Specific Goals (Examples)

- Improve management of insects, diseases, nematodes, and weeds.
- Improve diagnostic abilities (recognize insect, disease, and weed pests *and* distinguish from agronomic imbalances).
- Identify key pests and develop pest profiles for each.
- Improve fertilizer practices ("spoon feed" more effectively; use slow- and fast-release nitrogen sources wisely).
- Improve irrigation system.
- Increase use of native or well-adapted plants on and around the golf course.
- Improve records of golf course condition throughout the year (pest and disease activity, agronomic conditions).

Expected Results (Examples)

- Improved quality of putting greens.
- Improved "success" at managing key pests.
- Make more educated decisions regarding selection of control options.

Figure 12.4. The Orchards Golf Course, South Hadley, Massachusetts. (Courtesy G.L. Schumann.)

The following lists provide examples of some of the areas often discussed in a policy statement. Some areas require more detail than others, including some background information and specific concerns.

Cultural Practices

Mowing Practices

- Use of vertical cutting.
- Use of lightweight mowers.
- Modified patterns to reduce soil compaction.
- Skip "cleanup passes" occasionally to reduce soil compaction.
- Keep mower blades sharp and properly adjusted.
- Use rollers occasionally to maintain putting speed without requiring an additional mowing.
- Height of cut.

Irrigation Practices

- Frequency and duration (syringing vs. soaking).
- Amount of water to be applied.
- Water source and quality.

Fertilization

- Understand seasonal needs.
- Nitrogen, phosphorus, and potassium balance.
- Use of slow- and fast-release sources of nitrogen.
- Test soil and plant tissue regularly and adjust fertilization accordingly.

Figure 12.5. Early morning irrigation. (Courtesy P.P. Cobb.)

Air Circulation

- Remove or prune key trees and landscape plants.
- Use of fans during hot, humid periods.

General Agronomics

- Identify localized dry spots and begin to amend soil conditions.
- Improve drainage.
- Pick up plant debris regularly.
- Dump clippings well away from the turf area.
- Topdress as appropriate.
- Overseed bare or thin areas (Figure 12.6).

Selection of Plant Material

- Select turf species and cultivars adapted to local conditions. Use quality seed and sprig sources.
- Select trees and other plants adapted to local conditions.
- Use native grasses and wildflowers to reduce water requirements and enhance visual appeal.

Manage Traffic Patterns

- Install cart paths where appropriate.
- Use signs to direct traffic where desired.
- Develop pattern of hole placements, so traffic does not enter and leave the green at the same point day after day.

Figure 12.6. Overseeding with improved cultivars. (Courtesy F.D. Dinelli.)

Pest Management

Identify Key Pests

- Problems on key areas (greens, approaches, fairways).
- Scout training requirements.
- Pest identification resources.

Develop Pest Profiles for Each Pest

- Life cycle.
- Sampling techniques.
- Tolerance thresholds.
- Cultural conditions that favor pest.
- Biological control options and timing.
- Chemical control options and timing.

Recordkeeping

- Pest populations *before* control action is taken.
- Weather records.
- Fertilizer, biological control, and chemical control applications.
- Pest populations *after* control action is completed.

Selecting Management Alternatives

Cultural

- Are there resistant turfgrass species or cultivars?
- Are there cultural practices that disrupt potential pests or pathogens or put them at a competitive disadvantage?
- Optimize agronomic conditions so the turf can best withstand pest pressure.

Biological

- Are there biological control alternatives?
- How consistent or reliable are they?
- Are there special handling concerns?
- What is the timing of application and need for water before or after application?

Chemical

- Are there environmental concerns (runoff, leaching, volatility)?
- Are there chemical control alternatives?
- How consistent or reliable are they?
- Timing of application.
- Equipment needs.

Measuring Results

Sample pest populations or record initial disease damage to determine whether a control action is necessary. After a control action has been completed, determine whether the problem has been controlled and if the level of control is satisfactory to you *and* the golfers.

- What was expected? (100% eradication is not reasonable or possible.)
- What would you do differently next time?
- How many hours of labor does scouting require?
- How many pesticide applications were eliminated as a result of scouting and using thresholds?
- How receptive have the golfers been to the program?
- What forms of communication have been most effective with golfers?
  - newsletters
  - signs at the pro shop
  - individual conversations

Figure 12.7. Pruning tree roots from fairways. (Courtesy F.D. Dinelli.)

Priorities

Which areas will be incorporated in the earliest phases?

What pest problems should be emphasized in the early stages of IPM applications?

Who will scout and maintain records?

What areas and pest problems will be added as resources and confidence increase?

Who Develops the Policy Statement?

IPM statements are usually developed by a superintendent after the idea is discussed with the board of directors, the greens committee, or whoever the ultimate decision makers are at your golf course. Situations vary, but input from these decision makers is often sought by superintendents. Once the policy statement is accepted and a plan is written, it is distributed to boards, committees, or other groups charged with approving the program. Superintendents may make a formal presentation to the committee or board.

Communication can determine the success or failure of an IPM program just as much as scouting or the lack thereof. Frequent reporting on status and progress helps the superintendent to get credit for the good, common sense approach that IPM offers.

Potential Benefits

• Written guidelines specific to, yet flexible for, your situation. A written statement reduces misunderstandings between the superintendent, the golfers, and course officials.

Figure 12.8. What do you want to achieve in the next five years? (Courtesy P.P. Cobb.)

- Improved communication with and support from course officials, golfers, and staff.
- Good public relations through communication of efforts and results of efforts with government agencies, the media, homeowner groups, and wildlife organizations.

SAMPLE POLICY STATEMENT

The following policy statement was contributed by Mr. Tim Hiers, CGCS, of Collier's Reserve Golf Course in Naples, Florida.

COLLIER'S RESERVE

Integrated Plant Management Program

Collier's Reserve golf course maintenance philosophy is geared toward enhancing the Integrated Plant Management (IPM) concept. Technically stated, IPM is reducing pesticide, fertilizer, and water usage over time by being aware of and practicing the following:

I. CULTURAL PRACTICES

    A. Vertical cutting fairway — not only provides healthier grass, but also increases the effectiveness of pesticides. A grass that has too much thatch can actually tie up pesticides and prevent them from getting to the target pest. By maintaining the right amount of thatch, pesticides can be effective against target pests while circumventing leaching below the root zone and avoiding a contamination problem. Utilizing pesticides more effectively reduces their usage.

B. **Tree removal and trimming** — Removing and/or trimming selected trees increases sunlight and air circulation to the turf. Both of these factors are critical in maintaining healthy turf. Excessive shade and poor air circulation not only weaken turf, but are directly correlated with higher disease occurrence. By reducing the factors that contribute to disease, we can reduce pesticide applications. In some cases, we may remove turf where it is not needed and plant trees and/or native or well-adapted vegetation. Judicious root pruning of adjacent trees can also reduce stress on turfgrass caused by expanding tree roots. We have also established a tree planting program. For every tree that dies we are replacing it with three trees of the same type. The first stage of installing lightning protection on key trees has been completed.

C. **Plant conditioning** — Establishing a comprehensive preventive maintenance program and equipment replacement schedule enables us to mow and maintain grass more efficiently. Therefore, the grass requires less fertilizer to maintain adequate color. For example: maintaining sharp and accurately adjusted mowing blades assists in maintaining healthy plant tissue and roots. Grass mowed with dull blades incurs significant damage from tearing, which produces open wounds, inviting disease and reducing root growth.

Damaged grass plants are more susceptible to insect and cart traffic damage, and also show poor assimilation of available fertilizer and water. Another example of plant conditioning concerns mowing frequency. Having adequate and well-maintained equipment means we can mow grass on a specific schedule. Grass allowed to grow too long suffers severe damage when finally mowed. A general rule of thumb is to never cut off more than 30% of the aboveground plant. Proper equipment makes this possible.

D. **Controlling cart traffic** — Installing adequate cart paths reduces turf and soil damage caused by carts. Soil compaction (caused by cart traffic) results in:

- poor oxygen and gas exchange
- restricted water percolation and increased water runoff (wasted water)
- slower infiltration of fertilizer, therefore limiting its effectiveness
- increased weed germination
- thinner, unhealthy turf

Again, a healthy turf requires less pesticides.

E. Improved drainage — Improved drainage decreases soil compaction and increases turf health.

F. General maintenance — Giving turf constant care keeps it in a more balanced condition. Daily debris pickup enhances course aesthetics and allows the equipment operator to do his job more efficiently. Example: Mower operators must get off their machines to move debris because it cannot be mowed over. (Debris = limbs, pine cones, etc.)

Green and fairway aerification with topdressing reduces stress from seasonal traffic. Frequent mowing helps bermudagrass compete with unwanted weeds.

II. COMPREHENSIVE SOIL TESTING

Accurate analysis and forecasting of fertility needs allows us to avoid applying unneeded components. It also means getting the most from our fertilizer dollar, plus a healthy grass plant. A healthier plant (not too weak or too lush) requires less pesticide. Specific pH testing provides amendment recommendations that balance the soil and facilitate proper fertilizer usage.

III. IPM SPECIALIST

The IPM Specialist maintains a Florida Restricted Pesticides license. In addition to on-the-job training, attending at least one seminar per year related to proper pesticide usage is mandatory. Videos (purchased/rented) related to safe and proper pesticide usage are made available for viewing. Technical materials that discuss safe and proper pesticide use for all materials used are always on file. (Experts in turf management and pest control are utilized as needed.)

Pulling weeds also helps to reduce pesticide use. All of our staff, including top management, thoroughly understands the concept of IPM, its goals, and how it relates to cultural practices.

A. Pest Threshold Tolerance Levels

Over a period of time we have learned the threshold level for grass plant tolerance of certain pests. For example: Beetle grubs that feed on grass roots are devastating at 12–14 grubs per square foot. Grass plants seem to tolerate 3–5 grubs per square foot. Therefore, we probably would not treat at the lower number, but would certainly treat at the higher number. The same approach is used on different pests, but completely different threshold numbers are applied according to the type of pest.

B. Pesticide Application Timing

Timing is one of several critical factors in reducing pesticide applications and getting maximum results from that application. For example: Applying insecticide/nematicide in early May, we control mole crickets, just hatching from their eggs, and kill nematodes hindering grass roots. Application at any other time would not be nearly as effective. Note: We anticipate our IPM Program may reduce or eliminate the necessity of this pesticide application.

C. Pesticide Application Techniques and Rotation

Calibration of application equipment and rotation of pesticides are critical to obtain maximum results. Miscalculations in application dosage can result in turf and environmental damage. Over- or underdoses can contribute to pests passing on pesticide tolerance to their future generations. Rotation of pesticide types can significantly reduce the incidence of pesticide tolerance in insects and pathogens. Altering the pH of the water carrying the pesticide can also dramatically increase its efficacy. As an example: Some organophosphate insecticides' effectiveness is severely reduced in high pH water. Adding citric acid to the water, which lowers the water pH, can increase the pesticide's efficacy as much as 30–50%.

Nighttime or late evening application of some pesticides can produce the following positive benefits:

- Improved results due to reduced exposure to sunlight, which has a debilitating effect on pesticides.
- Safer conditions to applicator due to cooler temperatures. (Certain pesticides are more volatile during warmer temperatures.)
- Reduced exposure to certain wildlife, such as most birds, squirrels, etc., because their activity is minimal at night.
- Significant reduction in wind speed, making application more effective, and reducing the chances of drift.
- Increased efficacy of application. Many turf insects surface and feed at night when most birds and other animals (pets) are not active.

Using nozzles with a sophisticated shielding system allows spraying on windy days and eliminates all wind drift. It also makes application more effective and safer.

One application technique that reduces potential harmful effects on wildlife or fish is to anticipate a hard 2-in. (5 cm) rain immediately after pesticide application. For example: When making applications near a body of water, rather than treat the whole area, treat only a portion and water it immediately; then several days later, treat another section in the same manner until, eventually, the whole area is treated. This significantly reduces the amount of material that could enter a lake or stream in the event of an unexpected hard rain after application.

IV. Optimum Irrigation Application

This can only be achieved by installing a state-of-the-art computer-operated irrigation system. State-of-the-art has changed several times in the past ten years. Significant reductions in pesticide usage, fertilizer applications, electricity costs, water usage, and even manpower can be achieved by using the most up-to-date system available. Utilizing a computer-efficient, low-pressure irrigation system (low-pressure is less affected by wind) and site-specific heads allows for low water use and maximum coverage. Optimum water usage means a decrease in:

- soil compaction
- fertilizer leaching
- disease susceptibility
- wear and tear on pumps and irrigation system
- weed population
- insect population

A modern system also allows irrigation according to evapotranspiration rates and in a condensed amount of time. We expect to see 18 holes irrigated in 6 to 8 hours. Some golf courses with a less modern irrigation system may need as much as 14 hours to irrigate 18 holes. A shorter irrigation cycle allows us to start the system later in the night, giving more time for rain. Also, reduced irrigation time reduces inconvenience and irritation to our golfing members.

V. Irrigation Water Quality

Quality irrigation water enhances the effectiveness of pesticides and fertilizers and requires less water to get desired results than if you were using poor quality water. Good quality water reduces potential leaching and electrical consumption. Example: a water high in pH (7.9) and very hard can be made softer (and therefore able to infiltrate the soil more efficiently) by lowering the pH with a safe additive, which also enhances the effectiveness of pesticides.

VI. Biostimulants and Biological Controls

We intend to use, and experiment with, both of the following sources:

- **Biostimulants** — These natural products are used to improve the health of the soil, increase microbial activity, and improve the cation exchange capacity. The net result of this is that the soil is better able to store nutrients, filter pesticides, and make the plants more proficient at assimilating fertilizers and water.

- **Biological Controls** — We are using and experimenting with different forms of biological controls to replace pesticides wherever practical. Some courses (including Collier's Reserve) are working with a nematode (a parasitic, microscopic worm) that — once it contaminates a mole cricket (with a bacterium) — will eventually kill the cricket.

VII. FERTILIZER SELECTION

The use of slow-release fertilizers such as IBDU provides these positive benefits.

- By their very definition, there is little or no nitrate leaching with slow-release fertilizer.
- Because the fertilizer is released slowly, the grass is not subject to large flushes of growth.
- Slow-release fertilizers supply grass with nutrients over a longer period of time, and reduce frequency and cost of fertilizer application.

VII. GRASS TYPE SELECTION

Research has been under way for several years to discover or produce grasses that are more pest-tolerant and use less water and fertilizer. During construction of our course, a concerted effort was made to avoid grasses, plants, or situations that would create a higher dependency on pesticides.

IX. MISCELLANEOUS

Computer-controlled weather stations give us the ability to produce accurate records on various levels, which will allow us to manage our pesticides, water, and fertilizers more efficiently.

X. WILDFLOWERS AND INDIGENOUS VEGETATION

Where it is practical and functional, we will install wildflowers or native or well-adapted vegetation rather than turf. To date, approximately 500,000 plants (up to 12 different species) have been installed on the property. Once established, these flowers or vegetation require little, if any, supplemental water, fertilizer, or pesticides. They enhance the surrounding turf, reduce maintenance costs, and provide diverse habitat for plants, animals, birds, and butterflies.

Conscientious golf course superintendents have practiced the elements of IPM for at least 50 years. Only recently was the term IPM defined to specifically identify this ongoing form of judicious resource management and environmental care. Because golf course superintendents are challenged with environmental compliance, competitive resource management, and demands for premium playing conditions, the concepts and benefits of IPM are being brought into full light while simultaneously highlighting the skills and concerns of these stewards of recreational lands.

IPM demonstrates to a concerned public that knowledgeable golf course superintendents actually enhance and protect our environment, and gives the experienced superintendent the opportunity to be a leader and educate the public in techniques for proper resource and environmental management. IPM is not a trendy term; it is just plain, good ol' common sense, great fore-planning and consistent, disciplined efforts.

— Tim Hiers, CGCS, Collier's Reserve, Naples, Florida

FURTHER READING

Audubon Society of New York. *The Audubon Cooperative Sanctuary System*, The Audubon Society of New York State, Selkirk, NY.

Broccolo, L.R. An Award Winning Management Plan, in *Handbook of Integrated Pest Management of Turf and Ornamentals*, Leslie, A.R., Ed., Lewis Publishers, Boca Raton, FL, 1994.

Bruneau, A.H., J.E. Watkins, and R.L. Brandenburg. Integrated Pest Management, in *Turfgrass*, Agronomy Monograph No. 32. Waddington, D.V., R.N. Carrow, and R.C. Shearman, Eds. ASA, CSSA, SSSA Publishers, Madison, WI, 1992.

Eskelson, D. Implementing IPM Strategies. *Golf Course Management*. 60(2):68–75, 1992.

Rhay, T. Avoid IPM Implementation Pitfalls, in *Handbook of Integrated Pest Management of Turf and Ornamentals*, Leslie, A.R., Ed., Lewis Publishers, Boca Raton, FL, 1994.

CHAPTER 13

IPM REGIONAL PORTRAITS

Practicing golf course superintendents from four regions of the United States have contributed the following summaries of their IPM programs. They are all using time-tested and well-known strategies as well as innovative practices *specific* to their own golf courses. Each of these individuals is an excellent example of the dedication and professionalism that are the hallmarks of successful and respected superintendents. The authors of this book know many such superintendents, but only a few could be featured here. We salute the energy, intelligence, and creativity with which golf course superintendents approach their profession.

SOUTHEAST

Darren Davis
Golf Course Superintendent
Old Florida Golf Club
Naples, Florida

[Condensed from a complete document]

The definition of Integrated Pest Management (IPM) at Olde Florida is the control of pests (insects, diseases, and weeds) utilizing all control methods available to us. This includes cultural (maintaining healthy turfgrass), mechanical (removal, without the use of chemicals), and finally chemical methods. When chemicals are deemed necessary, they are used judiciously and only after a threshold level of damage has been observed. The threshold level varies depending on the area where the damage occurs. The greens are always priority one. The next highest level of maintenance performed is on the tees, followed by the fairways, and finally the rough. Outside the roughs we attempt to maintain only native grasses, shrubs, and trees that require little to no maintenance.

The philosophy of the management at Olde Florida is to have quality, educated, trained people. These educated turf managers are extra sets of eyes and ears that continually inspect and monitor the golf course. If a problem is found, a Pesticide Management Methodology is used to determine the plan of action taken. This Methodology plan is an itemized checklist that includes monitoring and mapping pest populations, action decision making, review of product labels

Figure 13.1. Superintendent Darren Davis, Olde Florida Golf Club. (Courtesy D. Davis.)

and material safety data sheets, correct application procedures (including calibration), container disposal and equipment cleaning, recordkeeping, and evaluations of effectiveness. All members of the management staff read and sign the document. It is then posted for review.

Cultural Control Methods

Our goal is to provide for our membership the most dense, vigorous, healthy turf possible with the funds we have to work with. The best defense against pests is a healthy stand of turfgrass.

Greens and tees are aerified, vertically mowed, and topdressed. Aerification on greens and tees includes use of walk-behind core aerification equipment during periods of least play (May to October), and water injection aerification during periods of most play (November to April). Sand topdressing is applied after cores are removed, or lightly at other times. Vertical mowing is done using a walk-behind unit or a triplex unit with vertical mowing reels, depending on the time of year.

Fairways at Olde Florida receive all the same cultural methods as greens and tees. The main difference is the size of the machines used. Fairway aerification includes use of a core aerator during the growing season (May to September), and during the heavier play months (November to April) a spiker is used. Fairway vertical mowing is performed two or three times a year. Fairway topdressing with sand is a new practice that will be done annually.

Roughs are treated very similarly to the other turfgrass areas on the golf course: aerification, spiking, vertical mowing, etc. Roughs do not receive a blanket topdressing application. The only topdressing the rough receives for thatch control is the soil that is applied when the aerification cores are broken up.

Weed removal: The crew members all pull weeds as they have time (waiting on play, etc.). The management staff pulls weeds daily. In fact, it is in their written job descriptions. The Assistant Superintendent pulls a minimum of 10 a day, the IPM Specialist a minimum of 20, the Irrigation Technician pulls 10, the Head Equipment Technician pulls 10, the Assistant Equipment Technicians pull 5, and the Superintendent a minimum of 5. If 10 people pull 10 weeds a day, 5 days a week, year round, we will have pulled 26,000 weeds.

Turf stress (traffic, carts, and mowing heights): During the cooler months, when the grass is not growing as aggressively, the maintenance staff strategically locates cart directional signs to divert the traffic. Maintenance staff uses service roads and natural areas and avoids driving on the turfgrass whenever possible. The theme at Olde Florida is a traditional golf course. This includes a caddie program, and golfers are encouraged to walk. This greatly reduces the cart traffic and consequent wear.

Mowing heights for each area of the golf course fluctuate year round, depending on the time of year, amount of play, or other factors. Our goal is adjusting heights to maintain optimum playing conditions while keeping the health of the turfgrass a top priority. Double cutting and rolling are two methods used on the greens to maintain speed without lowering the height of cut excessively. Solid rollers are also used — instead of grooved rollers — during stress periods to avoid wear.

Biological Control Methods

Biological control at Olde Florida includes the following:

- Providing test sites for biological fertilizers and other soil amendments, insect-parasitic nematodes, and new turfgrass species.
- Installation of various bird nesting structures.
- Choice of turf species (hybrid bermudagrasses) adapted to South Florida, and use of various cultivars for greens, tees, etc.
- Use of natural organic fertilizers and pesticides where possible.

Chemical Control Methods

All of the pesticides applied at Olde Florida Golf Club are on a curative basis. Preventive applications of herbicides, insecticides, nematicides, or fungicides are *not* done. If a pest population has reached a threshold level and a compound is deemed necessary, strict guidelines are followed in the application of the product.

One example is mole crickets. During the fall, winter, and spring, the majority of the mole cricket activity is suppressed by injecting individual burrows. Our goal is not complete eradication. On the tees, greens, and approaches, a one-gallon sprayer is used; on fairways, a 15-gallon sprayer with hand wand is used to treat the individual burrows. We have found by staying on top of the activity in the off-peak season, our over the top applications to "hot spots" are limited. Soap flushes are also performed on our normal hot spots beginning in late February. The areas of heaviest activity during the summer are marked and recorded, and these are the areas where we initiate soap flushes during the spring. If adults are brought up, we dissect their bodies and inspect for eggs. When nymphs are found, we wait a couple of weeks to ensure that the majority of the eggs have hatched. Then the typical hot spots are treated to control as many of the nymphs as possible.

Employee Education and Training

Education is an ongoing process for the superintendent and the crew. Training at Old Florida includes:

- Cooperative effort with another superintendent in development of video training tapes for the golf course maintenance crew (Superintendents' Video Workshop).
- Hands-on training individually or in small groups.
- Encouragement of continuing education of staff through community college classes and local and regional seminars.

IPM Center

The IPM building is one of three buildings in the maintenance compound. It is located in an open area with good light and air circulation, elevated above the surrounding area to prevent runoff into the building or mix/load area. Features include:

- Ventilation fan to remove fumes (discharge out of the rear of the building) and aid cooling, turned on before entering building.
- Concrete block structure, 25 feet by 35 feet, with a poured 6-inch concrete curb to contain potential spills. The concrete is sealed with a stain/sealer for easy spill visibility and cleanup. Keys are issued only to authorized people. A fire extinguisher and telephone are located in quick-access areas.
- Products and tools stored on epoxy-coated steel shelving or in plastic containers. Products are stored separately according to their intended use (herbicide, insecticide, etc.), and are organized according to their formulation. Powders and granules are stored on a higher shelf than liquids.

- An 8-foot roll-up door on one side of the building for easy access for deliveries away from the mix/load area. The sprayer is backed into the IPM building and stored there at night.
- The mix/load area is attached to the building but separated by a block wall. The overhead fill line leaves an "air gap" between the water supply line and the sprayer tank. If spills occur, materials are contained in this area, hosed down into a sump, and pumped back into the spray tank. Water used for cleaning equipment and for an emergency eye wash is also contained in this way.

NORTHEAST

Charles T. Passios, CGCS
Manager of Golf Course and Grounds
The Nantucket Golf Club
Nantucket Island, Massachusetts

The following is the conceptual IPM approach that was a proven plan at the Hyannisport Club and will be used at the Nantucket Golf Club, currently under construction.

IPM, in many cases, is an integrated approach to maintaining a certain level of acceptance of products such as landscapes, produce, conservation lands, and even human health, in a holistic sense. Our approach to golf course management isn't just pest management; it's property management. Integrated Property Management is the start to an all-around functional management strategy that will help ensure that your club's activities are productive, efficient, and environmentally sound. The first step is to look at all of the departmental functions of each area of the organization: what are their operational impacts, how can the impacts be minimized, and what are the plans for the future? The infrastructure (i.e., sewage treatment, waste removal, recycling, fuel storage, building safety, etc.) are major parts of the operational review, as potential impacts from these areas would be far more physically or environmentally damaging than nearly any operations of the golf course. Addressing these items will go a long way in the managing of costs, safety, and environmental integrity of many potentially overlooked areas of the property. New facilities are governed by permits that require Integrated Property Management, but this is an approach that should be considered by existing golf operations on a voluntary basis.

Hyannisport Club

Integrated Property Management was followed successfully at the Hyannisport Club and was recognized by the Audubon Society of New York State as the first Certified Audubon Sanctuary in New England. The Sanctuary Program requires that the club plan and implement proficiency in six areas that include: Wildlife & Habitat Management, Public Involvement, Environmental Planning, Integrated Pest Management, Water Conservation, and Water Quality Management, which together embrace the property management concept. Each management approach has a positive impact on the others, ultimately producing an overall product that has quality in playability, aesthetics, ecological enhancement, and efficiency.

IPM on the golf course follows the basic concepts. We continually scout the golf course for problem areas, record the findings in a scouting binder, and report to the supervisor on duty for followup. The supervisor then reviews the findings with the employee, considers the importance of the sighting, and views the site if needed. Once a problem is identified, all of the contributing factors are considered: acceptable threshold of damage, climatic conditions (changing or not), nature of the problem (nutritional, disease, insect, or other), and actions to be taken, if any. All decisions are followed by monitoring and documentation. This may seem time-consuming, but in most cases, items reported can be recorded without taking any outside action — i.e., letting nature take its course. As the program progresses, the documentation of occurrences will create a historical database that will eventually prepare the operation of the golf course with knowledge that can help anticipate problems and avoid repeated problems. An example would be that the #12 flag site is a hot spot for brown patch when conditions are right for disease development.

Having educated employees doesn't specifically mean that everyone needs to be an agronomist or an entomologist to run an effective IPM program on the course. It does mean, though, instilling in your employees the need to be aware of the quality that is expected, what the quality should look like, and to be aware of their surroundings. For example, your golf course's own natural residents, such as birds, will prove to be some of your best indicators of problems. Involving all of the employees will instill a sense of pride in accomplishing the end product. These general observations, along with those of the trained scouts (usually placement students as well as full-time staff) who actually look for signals of problems based on historical data, will equip the golf course IPM program for success.

IPM focuses on pest management, while our first focus is on plant management to produce a viable, healthy turf community. Cultural practices and getting back to basics are an important first step. Whether it is aerification, mowing practices, topdressing, nutrition, water management, or vertical mowing, every action will have a reaction. If done with plant health in mind, most problems will be limited. Biological controls are very important and effective, given the proper conditions and time to maintain acceptable thresholds. Organic fertilizers are incorporated into a nutritional approach that utilizes many different materials to address not only plant nutrition, but more importantly, soil nutrition. Water management is controlled to irrigate only where and when necessary, utilizing wetting agents to broaden the efficiency of the irrigation cycles. A dry, lean diet works very well for this coastal location. The key to an integrated approach is to have a large variety of products and cultural concepts available for use, which allows flexibility in addressing the needs on the course.

The bottom line for the integrated program at the Hyannisport Club is that the entire property is considered, along with the expectations of the product, while maintaining the integrity of this very ecologically sensitive seaside golf club.

The Nantucket Golf Club

As this is a golf club under construction in the '90s, you know that the permitting process has been extensive, especially with the location on an island 27 miles southeast of Cape Cod, Massachusetts. With the permitting came environmental impact statements dealing with roads, buildings, traffic, sewage treatment, water quality, industrial management, golf course management, and natural habitat restoration. The permits helped to develop all of the plans for structures, environmental protection, endangered species protection/enhancement, sewage management, golf course management — which together sound like IPM, Integrated Property Management. This club is not only focused on a world class golf experience, but it is committed to low impact on the land, preserving/restoring state endangered grasslands, and participating in partnership with statewide groups in re-establishing habitat for the endangered Harrier Hawk (Marsh Hawk). Among all this planning is the actual permit, which includes the Integrated Golf Course Management Plan by Michael J. O'Connor, CGCS, Turf Agronomist for Environmental Turf Service. Though most would say that such plans are developed to get permits, this plan is actually stated in the permit that governs the management of the golf course. The only item missing is the actual input by the manager of the property, who joined the team at a later date. Though the plan limits the flexibility of management, all permits may be revisited and amended as time passes and technology changes.

We are using the same approaches to bring this golf course online as were used at the Hyannisport Club. Scouting will be the highest priority, especially as we bring along 90 acres of new turf, with another 60 acres of restored grasslands and endangered plant species. As listed in the Integrated Golf Course Management Plan (IGCMP), the management strategy includes the author's concept of IPM: **a containment strategy designed to manage, not eradicate, pest problems, consisting of ecologically sound practices to create a balance between pests and their naturally occurring predators.** Thresholds have been established for various pest populations, with a level of remedial actions based on a worst case scenario, to establish a study base in presenting an acceptable, though limited, list of turf care products. This study then provided the chemical tools — those with the least environmental impact — that would be allowed for this property. As already mentioned, the success of a solid IPM strategy is based on having vast flexibility in materials and approaches. Because of the limitations of the IGCMP, the cultural/holistic approach then becomes an even higher priority in the management of this golf course, which is the basis for all strong integrated programs.

The strategies listed for the Hyannisport Club will be integrated with the guidelines set forth in the Nantucket Golf Club management plan. Documentation will be of the highest priority as the turfgrass grows in and the stages of maturation proceed. The baseline that will be developed over time will become the operational guide in planning and managing this highly sensitive property. Part of the process includes a groundwater monitoring project that will document the activities of the club over time, creating baselines that support or don't support the management plan implementation, help create long-term strategies, and provide a barometer of management activities. The establishment of a grassland restoration program will become a case study of the effect of this type of development and provide information for similar projects in the future. As the actual implementation begins, the tools are in place for an even more extensive integrated program than we had at the previous club.

Philosophically, the approach is to let mother nature run her course, taking a kind of "wait and see" attitude. Reality, though, is that there is a level of expectation from the game itself that will require actions to be taken from time to time. IPM is a conceptual tool that most often works well, and other times doesn't. As our knowledge of the property expands, we will be well prepared to do the best that can be done.

WEST

Roger "Reed" Yenny, CGCS
Golf Course Superintendent
Mesa Verde Country Club
Costa Mesa, California

Mesa Verde Country Club opened in 1959 as part of a residential housing project. The golf course was purchased by the members in 1974 and has operated as a private 18-hole equity club since that time. The course covers nearly 150 acres, including 3 acres of greens, 3 acres of tees, 21 acres of fairways, and the remaining area in rough and clubhouse space. The greens were constructed from native soils and originally seeded to seaside creeping bentgrass. The majority of the course lies in the floodplain of the Santa Ana River bed, and is located approximately 3 miles inland from the Pacific Ocean. The soils range from a silty loam to heavy clays, except for several of the greens that have been reconstructed using sand-based root zones. Annual bluegrass is now the predominant turf species on the greens, and it does well most of the year in the

Figure 13.2. Annual bluegrass practice putting green at Mesa Verde with the clubhouse in the background. The yellow squares are plots of annual bluegrass treated with herbicide prior to bentgrass overseeding. (Courtesy L. Stowell.)

Figure 13.3. Jeff Menchinger, Assistant Superintendent (left) and Reed Yenny, Superintendent (right), Mesa Verde Country Club. (Courtesy L. Stowell.)

moderate climate. The majority of pesticide inputs are applied to green and fairway acreage.

The target of the Mesa Verde turfgrass management program is to provide the grass plant with the most desirable growth environment and to sustain our membership's golfing goals while minimizing environmental impacts and reducing the cost of management. The ideal turfgrass conditions for greens and fairways are:

Greens — annual bluegrass (*Poa annua*)

- Smooth surface for putting
- Moderate speed, 8–9 feet
- Green color
- Turf that is tolerant of variations in environmental conditions, traffic, insects, and disease

Fairways — kikuyugrass (*Pennisetum clandestinum*)

- Solid turf cover and firm soils for good ball lies
- Uniform throughout the course
- Fertility and growth regulation programs to reduce scalping, improve color, and reduce mowing and leaf clipping waste

Greens: Although pest management is a key component of the program at Mesa Verde, proper cultivation programs supersede pest management decisions. Without effective cultural management, IPM programs turn into programs that integrate different products for disease, insect, and weed controls that are frequently unnecessary. Cultural programs begin with the soil and end with the sharpness of mower blades.

The key cultural management components for greens include:

- Soil testing (spring and fall) to evaluate and adjust soil chemistry through application of amendment to match course soil chemical guidelines.
- Water testing and amendment with gypsum to correct the high sodium absorption ratio (SAR), low electrical conductivity (EC) water to improve infiltration.
- Weekly soil EC monitoring during the high evapotranspiration months and leaching to maintain a soil EC below 3.0 dS/m.
- During the summer, monthly shallow hollow core aeration (1.4 inch tines on 2x2 inch spacing) to improve gas exchange with the root zone.
- Vertical cutting as needed, to prevent excessive "puffiness" and thatch accumulation.
- Periodic topdressing to maintain a firm and smooth putting surface.
- Precision sharpened and maintained mowers.
- Application of foliar fertilizers during the summer when annual bluegrass roots are less than 1.5 inches long to meet the growth needs of the plant. Complete fertilizers are used at 1:1:1 ratios, including micronutrients. In the summer the system is essentially hydroponic because the roots do not extend deeply into the soil. Application rate

and frequency are adjusted to produce about 1 mower basket of clippings per 5,000 sq ft green per day.

- Large core aeration and deep aeration in the springtime, and topdressing to fill the holes with USGA specification sand. This system provides channels of low compaction and high water infiltration.
- Summer patch preventive fungicide applications begin when soil temperatures at 2 inches deep reach 75°F on three consecutive days. Demethylase inhibitor (DMI) fungicides are applied at monthly intervals (e.g., triadimefon at 1 oz/1000 sq ft delivered in 4 gal water/1000 sq ft) until mid to late June. At that time, temperatures are too high to treat annual bluegrass with DMI fungicides, and the benzimidazoles are used whenever summer patch symptoms reappear (e.g., thiophanate methyl at 4 oz/1000 sq ft in 4 gal water/1000 sq ft).
- Pythium blight and anthracnose control products are applied during the summer prior to leaching events when moisture levels will be excessive and conducive for disease.
- Winter disease control products are applied when the disease first occurs, primarily for Fusarium patch and brown patch. Preventive applications for winter diseases are not applied on a calendar basis.
- Insect populations are monitored weekly using a black light trap to help decide when to begin inspecting greens for insect damage. Insecticides are only applied when insects are found attacking the turf at levels that will interfere with golf play or result in turf stress and failure during the summer. Key insect pests are black cutworms, armyworms, and black turfgrass ataenius.

Fairways: Fairway management programs focus upon healthy soils to improve the competitiveness of the kikuyugrass against weeds and to improve kikuyugrass quality.

- Soluble fertilizers are applied on an as-needed basis to maintain healthy growth. Timing of application is adjusted to growth and clipping rates.
- During the rapid growth periods from spring through fall, a plant growth regulator (e.g., Primo) is applied to tighten up the turf canopy, improve ball lies, reduce scalping, and improve quality, in addition to reducing leaf clippings waste.
- Fungicides are only used as a spot treatment to control brown patch, which may occur during high rainfall years.
- Herbicides (e.g., simazine) are used to remove cool-season grass weeds (e.g., annual bluegrass).

MIDWEST

F. Dan Dinelli, CGCS
Golf Course Superintendent
North Shore Country Club
Glenview, Illinois

[Condensed from a complete document.]

My experiences and practices are based on 20 years at North Shore Country Club, located 20 miles north of Chicago. It is a temperate climate in hardiness zone 5. We basically have a heavy clay loam soil. The golf course was designed by H.S. Colt and C.H. Alison and built in 1924. We maintain tees and fairways on virgin soils, and the greens are based on push-up construction with a modified high sand/peat layer approximately 3 inches deep from topdressing. Grasses on greens, tees, and fairways are creeping bentgrass and annual bluegrass.

My approach to plant health care recognizes that the health of the plant depends on its environment and the interactions of a multitude of other organisms. The challenge is to understand these interactions and develop strategies to stimulate the environment to favor the desired plant. Tools used in the strategies formulated need to be economically and ecologically sound. Often multiple tactics are used to coordinate cultural, mechanical, biological, and chemical functions.

Everyone on a golf course has an active role in IPM. Golfers need to be educated about basic agronomic needs of the course. With this comes tolerance of management practices and respect. Beyond this more passive role, golfers directly contribute with proper ball mark and divot repair and utilizing "spikeless" golf shoes. We reach our golfers through newsletters, bulletin boards, and conversation.

Scouting and Monitoring

Intensive, regular monitoring is the most time-consuming and demanding practice in IPM. It is critical to detect and identify pests and potential problems as early as possible. This task is done at least twice a day. Part of our continuing education program for the crew is informative posters displayed in the shop, with videos and other references on pest identification and management. Scouting goes hand-in-hand with monitoring and written notes. In time, trends develop, "hot spots" emerge, and maps of these areas can be used for future reference.

Insect Trapping

We have used pheromone traps and a black light trap. Traps help us to better understand the population cycles and density of insects as well as to sched-

Figure 13.4. 14th Hole—North Shore Country Club. (Courtesy F.D. Dinelli.)

Figure 13.5. Metos Weather Station and indicator plants for phenology studies. (Courtesy F.D. Dinelli.)

ule scouting intensity. The black light trap has helped us track the local Japanese beetle population explosion. The steady increase in adults was confirmed in the steady increase of and damage caused by the grubs. We use the cutworm pheromone trap to capture the adult moth. We use this information to judge when to collect clippings and compost them offsite. The collected clippings yield the majority of eggs laid. This practice has reduced our insecticide applications. During course setup, the greens are assessed for holes, which can be spot-treated by a hand sprayer.

Degree-day models: We use the Metos weather station to calculate degree-days to help focus intense scouting for a particular insect and better target pesticide applications if needed. It can also be used to predict annual bluegrass flowering for the application of growth regulators.

Phenology

Because plants and insects share the physiological response to the accumulation of degree-days, field observations of plant activity can also help in determining insect and weed activity. An example is applying a pre-emergence herbicide for control of crabgrass when the bridal wreath spirea (*Spiraea X. Vanhouttei*) blooms. I have found that phenology is not only helpful but fun.

Key plants: We also use indicator plants as key plants. A bentgrass nursery of over 35 cultivars is maintained onsite with no plant protectants to help predict dollar spot and brown patch. Plots of perennial ryegrass are observed for Pythium blight.

Disease forecasting models: Our Metos weather station has three prediction models for turf diseases: Pythium blight, brown patch, and dollar spot. These predictive models are used as indicators of favorable environmental conditions for disease. They do not account for many other factors important in disease pressure. Ultimately, it is the turf manager who makes the decision on disease pressure vs. needed control.

Testing: Soil tests, periodic tissue testing, water testing, and disease diagnostic tests are done. In our annual operating budget we have a separate account just for testing fees.

Networking: Consulting with other superintendents and university professionals is very helpful.

Computers: We use computers in many ways: access to weather data and degree-day figures, disease forecasting models, and evapotranspiration. Two complete sets of drawings are scanned into our computer hole by hole. One set has our irrigation and drainage; the other is used to map "hot spots." The computer is also used to go online to superintendents' bulletin boards and several other services, including the Turfgrass Information Center at Michigan State University.

Cultural Methods

The following is a brief summary of cultural practices that I feel have made a significant favorable impact under our growing conditions. By no means does this include all cultural methods used:

- Proper pruning and thinning of trees.
- Overseeding with improved cultivars.
- Dew and guttation fluid removed daily.

- Vertical cutting is done each time the greens are mowed.
- Rolling greens after mowing is done prior to golf events. This allows faster roll without lower mowing heights.
- Root pruning of trees

Fertility management: The following is our basic fertility program. Though we constantly fine tune our program, I feel the products used have given us a great life support system for plant health and essential soil microorganisms required to build a strong, healthy, aggressively growing plant while improving the productivity of the soil naturally.

- Annual soil tests.
- Natural and organic fertilizers — activated sewage sludge, hydrolyzed feather meal, meat meal, bone meal, poultry meal, blood meal, fish meal, langbeinite, and sunflower seed hull ash. These biostimulants enhance biological activity as well as being a source of plant nutrients.
- Foliar sprays are used as needed with readily available elements.
- Seaweed extract as a source of cytokinin.
- Yard waste compost as a soil amendment, fertilizer, and disease suppressant on fairways has resulted in fewer localized dry spots, reduced thatch, and increased earthworm activity.

Cultivation: On greens, soil compaction is relieved by deep shatter tining with half-inch tines penetrating 10 inches deep. Holes are left open. Mid-season cultivation on greens and tees is done by high-pressure water injection as needed.

On tees, fairways, and roughs, coring is done spring and fall. On tees, the cores are removed. On fairways and roughs, the cores are broken up and worked back into the thatch and soil profile. On fairways, we have included a topdressing of yard waste compost as part of the operation.

Irrigation: Information from our weather station, i.e., soil moisture sensor and evapotranspiration (E.T.), combined with daily field monitoring, dictates our irrigation needs. Several additives are injected into our irrigation system, including surfactants to aid in water retention and percolation and urea/sulfuric acid to manage high bicarbonate levels. A third injection system applies bacteria for disease suppression.

Chemical Methods and Considerations

Our plant protectant program is designed to minimize the use of chemicals. When pesticides are used, they are chosen carefully and used according to label instructions. Considerations are made on how it may affect biologicals, especially the microorganisms we are using. Every effort is made to maximize the

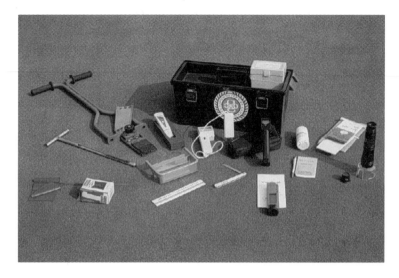

Figure 13.6. IPM toolbox. (Courtesy F.D. Dinelli.)

chemical's use. pH is tested to ensure that alkaline hydrolysis of the pesticide is minimized. Covered spray booms are used, equipped with flat-fan, high-pressure nozzles. This ensures good spray distribution deep into the sward. Being covered, drift is prevented, putting all the product on the target.

With the exception of putting greens and some diseases, I adhere to a curative chemical program. What has made the largest impact on reducing chemical use is my attitude toward diseases. Many times the symptoms go away by microbial antagonism, immunity, or change in environmental conditions. *I have also learned that it was I who demanded the perfect disease-free turf, not the golfer.* Golfers do not recognize minor disease symptoms unless they are on the putting greens. Our program has largely moved to a preventive program by the use of cultural, biological, and biostimulant approaches. This has afforded us the ability to move to a curative chemical approach.

This change is challenging for several reasons. First, a more intimate understanding of the plant's ecosystem is needed to understand plant health care. Second, it is easier to budget for a preventive spray program. Finally, it is unnerving to monitor disease symptoms and take a "wait and see" approach.

Biological Practices and Control

A brief study of microbiology quickly demonstrates that microbial activity governs the world. My overall management of plant health care has grown from turfgrass management to turfgrass bionomics. The goal is to enrich microbial activity, enhance resident antagonists, and inoculate with antagonists to suppress diseases. Countless microorganisms exist, but few are commercially available. It is difficult to make generalizations or summarize microbial management. It is a dynamic science that I do not know enough about to make accurate broad statements. In the past, names like *Rhizoctonia, Fusarium, Typhula* meant plant diseases. Now science has discovered that species of *Rhizoctonia* control brown patch, *Fusarium* species control dollar spot, and *Typhula phacorrhiza* controls Typhula blight. The following is a list of organisms I have used: *Bacillus subtilus, B. licheniformes, B. megaterium, B. thuringiensis, Pseudomonas aureofaceans, P. cepacia, P. fluorescens, Trichoderma harzianum,* three proprietary strains of endomycorrhizal VAM, *Azospirillum brasilense,* endophytes, and *Steinernema riobravis.* I have seen good results with some of these organisms, and in other cases results were difficult to quantify. For organisms to be effective, we must maintain high enough populations. Often, frequent applications are needed to maintain high enough counts. I have used an irrigation injection system for two seasons (since 1995). Since the incorporation of this device, I now water early at night. Any free water on the plant is laced with antagonistic organisms suppressing plant pathogens. My experiences with biologicals as a whole have been favorable. However, there are more questions than answers at this time.

Greens, tees, and often fairways are disturbed sites. I look forward to and welcome the challenge as science moves from theory to function in restoring these sites for optimum turfgrass health that is in harmony with nature. Genetic modification of turfgrass cultivars teamed with management of favorable microbial populations is a long-term view of sustainable procedures in holistic plant health care.

If golfers only knew!

APPENDIX 1

SOURCES OF MAJOR IPM REFERENCES AND TRADE MAGAZINES

1. **American Phytopathological Society Press,** 3340 Pilot Knob Rd., St. Paul, MN 55121; phone: 1-800-328-7560.

   Clarke, B.B. and A.B. Gould, Eds. *Turfgrass Patch Diseases Caused by Ectotrophic Root-infecting Fungi*, 1993.

   Schumann, G.L. and J.D. MacDonald. *Turfgrass Diseases: Diagnosis and Management CD-ROM*, 1997.

   Smiley, R.W., P.H. Dernoeden, and B.B. Clarke. *Compendium of Turfgrass Diseases*, 1992.

   Annual publication of *Biological and Cultural Tests* and *Fungicide and Nematicide Tests*.

2. **Ann Arbor Press,** 121 South Main St., P.O. Box 310, Chelsea, MI 48118.

   Karnok, K.J. *Turfgrass Management Information Directory,* 1997.

   Potter, D.A. *Destructive Turfgrass Insects: Biology, Diagnosis, and Control,* 1997.

   Tani, T. and J.B Beard. *Color Atlas of Turfgrass Diseases,* 1997.

   Ann Arbor Press publishes a number of other turfgrass books.

3. **Avanstar Communications Inc.,** 7500 Old Oak Blvd., Cleveland, OH 44130-1830; phone: (218) 723-9477.

   Landscape Management (free to qualified persons)

   TurfGrass Trends

4. **The Audubon Cooperative Sanctuary System,** The Audubon Society of New York State, 46 Rarick Rd., Selkirk, NY 12158; phone: (518) 767-9051.

5. **Cornell University Press,** P.O. Box 250, Ithaca, NY, 14853; phone: (607) 277-2338.

   Tashiro, H. *Turfgrass Insects of the United States and Canada*, 1987.

   Ura, R.H., J.C. Neal, and J.M. DiTomaso. *Weeds of the Northeast* (in press)

6. **Entomological Society of America,** P.O. Box 177, Hyattsville, MD 20781-0177; phone: (301) 731-4535.

   Brandenburg, R.L. and M. G. Villani. *Handbook of Turfgrass Insect Pests,* 1995.

   Annual publication of *Arthropod Management Tests.*

7. **Golf Course Superintendents Association of America,** 1421 Research Park Dr., P.O. Box 927, Lawrence, KS 66044-0927; phone: 1-800-974-2722.

   Burpee, L.L. *A Guide to Integrated Control of Turfgrass Diseases. Vol. 1: Cool-Season Turfgrasses, Vol. 2: Warm-Season Turfgrasses,* 1993 and 1995.

   Golf Course Management magazine

   GCSAA Bookstore has numerous turf publications for sale.

8. **Intertec Publishing Corp.,** P.O. Box 12930, Overland Park, KS 66282-2930.

   Grounds Maintenance (free to qualified persons)

9. **IFAS Publications,** University of Florida, P.O. Box 110011, Gainesville, FL 32611-0011; phone (352) 392-1764.

   Murphy, T.R., D.L. Colvin, R. Dickens, J.W. Everest, D. Hall, and L.B. McCarty. *Weeds of Southern Turfgrasses.*

   Unruh, J.B. and M.L. Elliott, Eds. *Best Management Practices for Florida Golf Courses,* 2nd edition, 1999.

10. **Krieger Publishing Co.,** P.O. Box 9542, Melbourne, FL, 32902-9542; phone: (407) 724-9542.

    Couch, H.B. *Diseases of Turfgrasses,* 1995.

11. **Lewis Publishers,** 2000 Corporate Blvd. NW, Boca Raton, FL 33431; phone: 1-800-272-7737.

    Leslie, A.R., Ed. *Handbook for Integrated Pest Management of Turf and Ornamentals,* 1994.

    Vargas, J. *Management of Turfgrass Diseases,* 1994.

    Watschke, T.L., P.H. Dernoeden, and D.J. Shetlar. *Managing Turfgrass Pests,* 1995.

12. **Plantsmen's Publications,** P.O. Box 1, Flossmoor, IL 60422

    Orton, D.A. *Coincide: The Orton System of Pest Management,* 1989 (timing pest management with ornamental plant development)

13. **Prentice-Hall, Inc.** phone: 1-800-947-7700.

   Beard, J.B. *Turfgrass: Science and Culture,* 1973.

   Fermanian, T.W., M.C. Shurtleff, R. Randell, H.T. Wilkinson, and P.L. Nixon. *Controlling Turfgrass Pests,* 1997.

14. **Sanders, Patricia,** 210 Buckhout Laboratory, University Park, PA 16802.

   Sanders, P. *The Microscope in Turfgrass Disease Diagnosis,* 1993.

15. **United States Golf Association,** Golf House, P.O. Box 708, Far Hills, NJ 07931; phone: (908) 234-2300.

   Beard, J.B. *Turfgrass Management for Golf Courses,* 1982.

   USGA Green Section Record

   USGA Bookstore has numerous turf publications for sale.

SCIENTIFIC NAMES OF COMMON TURFGRASSES, INSECTS PESTS, FUNGAL PATHOGENS AND WEEDS

Table 1. Golf Course Turfgrasses Listed in This Book.

Cool-season

Annual bluegrass	*Poa annua*
Colonial bentgrass	*Agrostis tenuis, A. capillaris*
Creeping bentgrass	*Agrostis palustris, A. stolonifera*
Fine-leaf fescues	*Festuca rubra, F. ovina,* etc.
Kentucky bluegrass	*Poa pratensis*
Perennial ryegrass	*Lolium perenne*
Rough bluegrass	*Poa trivialis*
Tall fescue	*Festuca arundinacea*

Warm-season

Bermudagrass, common	*Cynodon dactylon*
Bermudagrass, hybrid	*Cynodon dactylon X. C. transvaalensis*
Kikuyugrass	*Pennisetum clandestinum*
St. Augustinegrass	*Stenotaphrum secundatum*
Zoysiagrass	*Zoysia japonica*

Table 2. Turfgrass Insect Pests Listed in This Book.

Annual bluegrass (Hyperodes) weevil	*Listronotus maculicollis*
Armyworm	*Pseudaletia unipuncta*
Billbugs	*Sphenophorus* spp.
Black turfgrass ataenius	*Ataenius spretulus*
Chinch bugs	*Blissus* spp.
Cutworms	
black	*Agrostis ipsilon*
bronzed	*Nephelodes minians*
variegated	*Peridroma saucia*
Fall armyworm	*Spodoptera frugiperda*
Greenbug	*Schizaphis graminum*
Ground pearls	*Margarodes meridionalis;* *Eumargarodes laingi*
Japanese beetle	*Popillia japonica*
Masked chafers	*Cyclocephala* spp.
May and June beetles	*Phyllophaga* spp.
Mole crickets	*Scapteriscus* spp.
Sod webworms	*Crambus* spp. and others
White grubs	
Green June beetle	*Cotinis nitida*
Japanese beetle	*Popillia japonica*
June beetle	*Phyllophaga* spp.
May beetle	*Phyllophaga* spp.
Oriental beetle	*Exomala orientalis*

Table 3. Turfgrass Fungal Diseases Listed in This Book.

Disease	Fungal Pathogen
Bermudagrass decline	*Gaeumannomyces graminis* var. *graminis*
Brown patch	*Rhizoctonia solani*
Dollar spot	*Sclerotinia homoeocarpa*
Fairy rings	numerous Basidiomycete fungi
Fusarium patch (pink snow mold)	*Microdochium nivale*
Leaf spot diseases	*"Helminthosporium"* fungi (old name); includes *Bipolaris, Drechslera,* and *Exserohilum* spp.
Necrotic ring spot	*Leptosphaeria korrae*
Pythium blight	*Pythium aphanidermatum* and other *Pythium* spp.
Red thread	*Laetisaria fuciformis*
Rusts	mostly *Puccinia* spp.
Southern blight	*Sclerotium rolfsii*
Stripe smut	*Ustilago striiformis*
Summer patch	*Magnaporthe poae*
Take-all patch	*Gaeumannomyces graminis* var. *avenae*
Typhula blight (gray snow mold)	*Typhula incarnata, T. ishikariensis*

Table 4. Turfgrass Weeds Listed in This Book.

Broadleaf weeds

Alligatorweed	*Alternanthera philoxeroides*
Burdock	*Arctium minus*
Buttonweed, Virginia	*Diodia virginiana*
Carrot, wild	*Daucus carota*
Chicory	*Cichorium intybus*
Chickweed, common	*Stellaria media*
Chickweed, mouse-ear	*Cerastium vulgatum*
Clover, sweet	*Melilotus* spp.
Clover, white	*Trifolium repens*
Dandelion	*Taraxacum officinale*
Henbit	*Lamium amplexicaule*
Hawksbeard, Asiatic	*Youngia japonica*
Knotweeds	*Polygonum* spp.
Medic, black; bird's foot trefoil	*Medicago* spp.
Pearlwort	*Sagina* spp.
Pigweed	*Amaranthus* spp.
Poorjoe	*Diodia teres*
Plantains	*Plantago* spp.
Pusley, Florida	*Richardia scabra*
Shepherd's purse	*Capsella bursa-pastoris*
Sorrell, red or sheep	*Rumex acetosella*
Speedwells	*Veronica* spp.
Spotted spurge	*Chamaesyce maculata*
Spurges	*Euphorbia* spp.
Teasel	*Dipsacus sylvestris*
Thistles	*Cirsium* spp., *Carduus* spp.
Woodsorrel	*Oxalis* spp.

Grassy weeds

Bluegrass, annual	*Poa annua*
Broomsedge	*Andropogon virginicus*
Crabgrass, hairy	*Digitaria sanguinalis*
Crabgrass, smooth	*Digitaria ischaemum*
Dallisgrass	*Paspalum dilitatum*
Goosegrass	*Eleusine indica*
Nimbleweed	*Muhlenbergia shreberi*
Orchardgrass	*Dactylis glomerata*
Quackgrass	*Agropyron repens*
Ryegrass	*Lolium* spp.
Sandbur	*Cenchrus pauciflorus*
Tall fescue	*Festuca arundinacea*

Sedges

Nutsedge, false	*Cyperus strigosus*
Nutsedge, yellow	*Cyperus esculentus*

GLOSSARY

Abiotic: non-living

Biocontrol/biological control: the use of a living organism or the product of a living organism to reduce a pest or pathogen population

Cation exchange capacity (CEC): the total amount of exchangeable cations that the soil can absorb; a measure of CEC reflects the ability of the soil to retain nutrients

Chlorosis/chlorotic: plants with yellow leaves

Compaction: pressure that packs soil particles together and reduces the soil pore space so drainage is impeded and oxygen supply to roots is reduced

Contact pesticide: see under fungicide or insecticide

Cross-resistance: resistance in an organism (fungus, insect, or weed) to chemically related compounds

Cuticle: the non-cellular outer covering of an insect or nematode

Degree-days: a method used to quantify the accumulation of heat units during a growing season and to predict development of a pest, plant, or other organism

Disease: disruption of normal growth and appearance of a plant due to interaction of the plant with a pathogen

Disorder: disruption of normal growth and appearance of a plant due to imbalances of certain physical or chemical requirements for turfgrass growth

Ecosystem: the entire collection of organisms interacting in an environment and affected by various environmental factors

ELISA: *e*nzyme-*l*inked *i*mmuno*s*orbent *a*ssay; a method of rapid identification using animal antibodies resulting in a color development.

Endophyte: fungus growing inside, but not at the expense of, plants; endophytic fungi can confer stress- and disease-tolerance to plants; endophytic fungi produce compounds that are toxic to surface-feeding insects and grazing livestock

Entomopathogen: an entity that causes disease in insects

Fertigation: application of fertilizers directly through an irrigation system

Fumigant: a chemical that produces a poisonous gas that diffuses through the soil to kill weeds, insect pests, fungi, nematodes, and other living organisms; sometimes used before establishment or re-establishment of turf

Fungicide: a chemical pesticide that suppresses growth of a fungus

   contact fungicide — protects surface of plant tissue; does not enter plant tissue; functions only in a protective manner

   localized-penetrant fungicide — enters plant tissue but does not move significantly away from that site; offers both protective and curative action against fungi

   systemic fungicide — enters plant tissue and is carried in xylem and/or phloem; most systemic fungicides move primarily upward in the xylem (acropetal penetrants)

Fungus/fungi: an organism composed of thread-like filaments that is unable to manufacture its own food and reproduces by asexual and/or sexual spores

Ground pearls: scale insects that live in the soil and feed by piercing tissue and extracting plant juice from grass roots; found in sandy soils of the southern United States

Guttation fluid: the liquid produced when water pressure from the roots forces plant water to exude through tiny leaf openings called hydathodes and through mowing wounds; this fluid contains important nutrients that favor the growth of fungal pathogens

Herbicide: a chemical pesticide that kills plants, especially weeds

   selective herbicide — is able to control the targeted weed plant without seriously affecting the growth of the desired plant

   non-selective herbicide — kills all plants

   pre-emergent herbicide — applied prior to seed germination of targeted weed

   post-emergent herbicide — applied to emerged weeds

IGR: insect growth regulator; a substance that affects an insect's developmental processes; some are used to interfere with the development of pest insects

Immunoassay: the use of animal antibodies to detect a parasite or substance of interest

Infection period: the combination of environmental factors (usually moisture and temperature) that results in successful infection by a parasite

Insect: an animal with an outer skeleton, three body regions, and six legs

Insecticide: a chemical pesticide that poisons or interferes with the growth processes of insects

> **contact insecticide** — an insecticide that the insect must physically encounter (absorb through the cuticle); most are nerve poisons

> **stomach poison** — must be ingested by the insect; disrupts digestive process or is absorbed through gut lining; some are nerve poisons

> **systemic insecticide** — enters plant tissue and is carried in xylem and/or phloem to other parts of the plant; often effective against insects with sucking mouthparts, particularly in ornamental plantings

Larva/larvae: immature stage of an insect which goes through complete metamorphosis, and bears no resemblance to the adult

Leaching: vertical (downward) movement of water (and pesticides dissolved or suspended in water) through the soil profile; can result in unintended movement of a pesticide from its initial point of application

Mandibles: jaw-like mouthparts of insects used to chew their food

Metamorphosis: the stages of development from an egg to an adult insect

> **complete metamorphosis** — immature insects do not resemble adults; egg, larva (immature), pupa, adult

> **incomplete or gradual metamorphosis** — immature insects closely resemble adults; egg, nymph (immature), adult

Mycelium/mycelia: the mass of thread-like filaments that comprise a fungus

Necrosis/necrotic: dead or dying leaves/plants

Nematicide: a chemical pesticide that suppresses growth and reproduction of nematodes

Nematode: a round worm (different from earthworms and other segmented worms); some are parasites of plants; entomopathogenic nematodes are used for biocontrol of insect pests

Nymph: immature stage of an insect with incomplete (gradual) metamorphosis; closely resembles the adult

Parasite: an organism that lives in or on another organism and obtains food from it for survival

Pathogen: an entity that causes disease, e.g., fungi, bacteria, viruses

pH: a number that expresses acidity or alkalinity (based on the logarithm of the reciprocal of the hydrogen ion concentration in gram-atoms per liter); a scale ranging from 0 to 14 (acidity to alkalinity); 7 is neutral

Phenology: the developmental stages of an organism over time

Pheromone: chemical produced by female insects to attract male insects; pheromones can be used in traps for IPM monitoring

Phloem: the conducting tissue of a plant that carries the products of photosynthesis (food) from the production site to the storage site; for turf, the primary production sites are leaves and the storage sites are stems and roots, so movement is primarily downward from leaves

Photosynthesis: process by which a plant utilizes water, carbon dioxide, and sunlight to produce carbohydrates (food) required for growth

Predator: an organism that searches out and attacks another organism

Pupa/pupae: the transformation (non-feeding) stage between a larva and an adult in insects with complete metamorphosis

Resistance or tolerance: the inherent genetic ability of a turfgrass species or cultivar to develop less disease or sustain less pest injury; refers also to the ability of a pest to not be killed by a pesticide after repeated use

Runoff: the lateral movement of water (and pesticides dissolved in water or soil particles suspended in water) on the surface; can result in unintended movement of a pesticide from its initial point of application

Salinity: the salt content in the soil or water

Saprophyte: an organism which obtains nutrients from dead organic matter

Sclerotium/sclerotia: a fungal survival structure; small dark mass of mycelium with a defined outer rind

Spore: a reproductive unit of a fungus important for survival and dispersal

Stylet: feeding structure used by nematodes and insects with piercing/sucking mouthparts

Systemic: moves within a plant's vascular tissue (xylem or phloem)

Thatch: the layer of organic materials that accumulates between the green, living vegetation of turf and the soil surface

Tolerance level/threshold level: pest populations or injury levels that trigger a management response; the acceptable level of injury varies depending on the area of a golf course and the decisions made by the owners, golfers, and superintendent

Toxin: poison

Volatility/volatilization: the transformation of a material (e.g., a pesticide) from a solid or liquid to a gaseous phase; similar to evaporation; can result in unintended movement of a pesticide from its initial point of application

Weed: a plant out of place

> **annual weed** — completes life cycle from seed to plant to seed in one year

> **biennial weed** — completes life cycle in two years, with flowering and seed production in the second year

> **perennial weed** — may flower and produce seed each year, but also survives for three or more years by vegetative means such as rhizomes or tubers

Xylem: the conducting tissue of a plant that carries water and minerals; movement is primarily upward from the roots to the leaves

INDEX